HOW TO STOP BEING STRESSED

THE S-I-M-P-L-E STEP-BY-STEP GUIDE TO RELAX YOUR MIND, OVERCOME NEGATIVITY, AND IMPROVE YOUR MENTAL HEALTH

SARRAH KAYE

Copyright © 2024 by Sarrah Kaye — All rights reserved.

The content contained within this book may not be reproduced, duplicated or transmitted in any form or by any electronic or mechanical means, including information storage and retrieval systems, without direct written permission from the author or the publisher, except for the use of brief quotations in a book review.

Under no circumstances will any blame or legal responsibility be held against the publisher, or author, for any damages, reparation, or monetary loss due to the information contained within this book, either directly or indirectly.

Legal notice:

This book is copyright protected. It is for personal use. You cannot amend, distribute, sell, use, quote or paraphrase any part, or the content within this book, without the consent of the author or publisher.

Disclaimer Notice:

Please note the information contained within this document is for educational and entertainment purposes only. All effort has been executed to present accurate, up to date, reliable, complete information. No warranties of any kind are declared or implied. Readers acknowledge that the author is not engaged in the rendering of legal, financial, medical or professional advice. The content within this book has been derived from various sources. Please consult a licensed professional before attempting any techniques outlined in this book.

By reading this document, the reader agrees that under no circumstances is the author responsible for any losses, direct or indirect, that are incurred as a result of the use of the information contained within this document, including, but not limited to, errors, omissions, or inaccuracies.

How To Stop Being Stressed

The S-I-M-P-L-E Step-By-Step Guide to Relax Your Mind, Overcome Negativity, and Improve Your Mental Health

By Sarrah Kaye

979-8340641656

To my husband, family, and friends, who have supported me throughout my stress-relieving journey with utmost patience, and helped me put what I've learnt into words and share it with the world.

A GIFT FOR YOU

To get you started on your journaling journey, I've put together this **30-day transformation journaling challenge workbook** for you.

If you would like to get your free copy, head over to https://subscribepage.io/transformationjournal or scan the QR code below.

CONTENTS

Introduction ... xi

1. WHAT IS STRESS? ... 1
   Types of Stress ... 2
   Emotional Symptoms of Stress ... 3
   Physiological Responses to Stress ... 5
   Focused Mode vs. Default Mode ... 8
   Your Instinctive Focus ... 10
   Stress and Neuroplasticity ... 12

2. WHAT ARE THE CAUSES OF STRESS? ... 14
   Everyday Causes of Stress ... 15
   Major Causes of Stress ... 17
   Traumatic Causes of Stress ... 20

3. WHAT ARE THE CONSEQUENCES OF STRESS? ... 23
   The Consequences of Acute Stress ... 24
   Acute Stress and Relationships ... 25
   The Consequences of Chronic Stress ... 28
   Stress and Your Brain ... 28
   Stress and Your Heart ... 30
   Stress and Weight Gain ... 31
   Stress and Your Immune System ... 32
   Stress and Cellular Aging ... 33

4. STRESS-RELIEF BREATHING ... 34
   Introduction to Breathwork ... 35
   How Breathwork Helps ... 35
   Techniques of Breathwork ... 37
   4-7-8 Breathing Technique ... 37
   Box Breathing ... 38
   Diaphragmatic Breathing ... 39
   Alternate Nostril Breathing ... 40

Pursed Lip Breathing	42
Lion's Breath	43
Five-Finger Breathing	44
Using Breathwork in Your Everyday Life	46

5. INTRAPERSONAL COMMUNICATION—SELF-TALK AND SELF-COMPASSION ... 49

Accepting Your Emotions	49
Strategies to Accept Your Emotions	51
Grounding Techniques	51
Emotion Surfing	52
Soften, Soothe, and Allow Technique	53
Benefits of Positive Self-Talk	54
Self-Talk Techniques	55
Perceived Stress Scale	55
Worst Case Scenario	56
Everything Happens for a Reason	57
The Control Issue	57
Will This Impact Me Tomorrow?	58
Self-Compassion	59

6. MINDFULNESS ... 61

What Is Mindfulness?	62
Benefits of Mindfulness	63
What State Are You Trying to Achieve?	64
The Observer	65
The "Being" Over "Doing" Solution	66
The Slow Down Captain	66
The Equanimity Teacher	66
The Non-Judgmental Friend	67
The Present Moment Ambassador	67
The Fear Replacement	67
Techniques to Achieve Mindfulness	68
Joyful Attention	68
Kind Attention	69
Refining Interpretations	71
Wheel of Awareness	72
The STOP Technique	73

Mindfulness Meditation	74
Benefits of Meditation	75
How to Meditate	77
7. PROGRESSIVE MUSCLE RELAXATION	79
What Is Progressive Muscle Relaxation?	79
Benefits of Progressive Muscle Relaxation	80
How Do You Do Progressive Muscle Relaxation?	81
Incorporating Progressive Muscle Relaxation Into Your Daily Life	83
8. LAUGHTER	84
Laughter Is the Best Medicine	85
Laughter and Stress	86
Short-Term Benefits of Laughter	87
Long-Term Benefits of Laughter	88
Incorporating Laughter Into Your Day-To-Day Life	89
Laughter Yoga	89
Funny Content	90
Laugh at Yourself	90
Laughter Exercise	91
Laughter as Part of Your Routine	91
Smile More	91
9. EXERCISE	93
Exercising and Stress	94
Benefits of Exercise	95
Reduces Stress	95
Improves Resilience	95
Boosts Cognitive Function	96
Improves Mood	96
Aerobic Exercise	97
Yoga and Pilates	98
Cat-Cow Pose (Marjaryasana to Bitilasana)	99
Child's Pose (Balasana)	100
Legs-Up-The-Wall Pose (Viparita Karani)	100
Corpse Pose (Savasana)	100
Building Exercise Into Your Routine	101

10. VISUALIZATION	103
What Is Visualization?	104
Benefits of Visualization	105
Techniques for Visualization	106
Blue Light Visualization	107
Goal Visualization	108
Color Breathing	108
Loving Kindness Visualization	109
Closed Window Visualization	109
Guided Imagery	110
11. THE POWER OF ROUTINE	112
The Importance of Routine	113
Tips to Set Up a Routine	114
Creating the Routine	114
Tips for a Morning Routine	115
Tips for a Night Routine	116
Adding Mindful Eating to Your Routine	117
Adding Proper Sleep Hygiene to Your Routine	118
Adding Journaling to Your Routine	120
Conclusion	123
Note from Author	127
References	129

INTRODUCTION

Your physical health and whether you are still alive in 10 years depends on the quality of your thoughts today.

- AMIT SOOD

These words by Amit Sood from *The Mayo Clinic Guide to Stress-Free Living* hold a profound truth that many of us overlook in the hustle and bustle of our daily lives: Stress isn't only a mental burden; it has a sneaky way of manifesting physically.

Think about it: You're going about your day, juggling work, family, and personal commitments, feeling the weight of the world on your shoulders. At first, it's all in your head—the racing thoughts, the constant worry, the never-ending to-do list. But soon enough, you start noticing changes in your body that you can't ignore. Maybe it's waking up to a face full of breakouts, stomach aches plaguing your mornings, or finding those extra pounds creeping onto your waistline. Perhaps it's those headaches so intense they force you back into bed in the middle of the day, leaving you drained and defeated.

If that sounds familiar, then you're in the right place. Let me guess, life has thrown you a curveball—or maybe several—and stress has become your unwelcome companion. Perhaps you've recently tied the knot, welcomed a new bundle of joy into the world, or found yourself uprooting your life in a move. Maybe it's the daily grind of work-related pressures, the aftermath of a relationship breakup, or the nerve-wracking excitement of starting your own business. The list could go on and on, couldn't it?

Perhaps, for you, stress isn't tied to any particular event—it's a constant presence lurking in the background of your life, ready to pounce at the slightest provocation. Traffic jams, looming deadlines, overdue bills, screaming children, partners who just don't seem to listen—anything and everything seems to set off that familiar knot in your stomach and that pounding in your head.

The truth is that stress doesn't discriminate. It doesn't care if you're a CEO, stay-at-home parent, student, or retiree. It can worm its way into every aspect of your life, wreaking havoc on your mental and physical well-being. And let's face it: In today's fast-paced world, stress seems almost inevitable.

Here's the thing: Stress doesn't have to rule your life. Your brain is an incredibly adaptable organ, capable of rewiring itself in response to new experiences and challenges. In other words, it's malleable—you can train it to handle stress in a more positive and productive way rather than getting stuck in a cycle of worry and rumination.

Take it from someone who's been there—I used to suffer from headaches and stomach aches almost daily. I spent years bouncing from specialist to specialist, trying to tackle each symptom individually, only to find myself trapped in a vicious cycle of stress and frustration. It wasn't until I took matters into my own hands, experimenting with different stress-management strategies and techniques and practicing patience, that I finally found relief.

Now, don't get me wrong—specialists can play a crucial role in your journey to better mental health. But ultimately, the power to break free from the grip of stress lies within you. This book will delve into the fascinating enigma of the brain and its role in orchestrating stress responses. It will discuss how, rather than tirelessly striving to your benefit, the brain can inadvertently amplify your stress levels beyond necessity. But more importantly, it will explore practical strategies and proven techniques to help you reduce your stress levels and transform your experience from overwhelming to manageable, even enjoyable.

Part 1 will explore the science behind stress, explaining what it is and how it impacts you mentally and physically. Part 2 will introduce you to the S-I-M-P-L-E framework: a comprehensive set of stress management strategies designed to empower you in your journey toward a more relaxed and joyful life. Each letter of the framework represents a key strategy you can implement to combat stress and build resilience:

- First up is **Stress-Relief Breathing**. This strategy will teach you how to use your breath as a powerful tool to calm your mind and body, even amid chaos.
- Next, you'll explore **Intrapersonal Communication**, also known as self-talk. You'll learn how to harness the power of your inner dialogue to challenge negative thoughts and cultivate a more positive mindset.
- Then, you'll delve into **Mindfulness**, a practice that involves bringing your awareness to the present moment. It's all about tuning in to your thoughts, feelings, and sensations with curiosity and acceptance.
- After that, you'll explore **Progressive Muscle Relaxation**, a technique that involves systematically tensing and relaxing different muscle groups to release physical tension and promote relaxation.
- Let's not forget about **Laughter**, a strategy that is often overlooked. You'll uncover the therapeutic benefits of

laughter and explore ways to incorporate more humor into your life.
- Finally, no stress management plan would be complete without **Exercise**. You'll discover how physical activity can not only improve your physical health but also boost your mood and reduce stress.

Finally, Part 3 will examine additional strategies to complement the ones outlined in the framework. These supplementary approaches will offer a well-rounded tool kit for managing stress in various situations and circumstances.

Together, these three parts will equip you with the knowledge and skills you need to take control of your stress and embrace a life filled with calm, clarity, and contentment.

I want to leave you with a sense of optimism and possibility. While consistency is key for long-term stress management success, the strategies in this book will also help you find relief in the heat of the moment. So, if you're tired of feeling overwhelmed and ready to reclaim your peace of mind, you've come to the right place.

1

WHAT IS STRESS?

IF YOU'VE PICKED up this book, chances are you're no stranger to stress. You know the drill—your heart races, your palms get sweaty, and suddenly, it feels like the weight of the world is sitting squarely on your shoulders. Sound familiar? But before you can overcome stress, you need to start with the basics: What is stress, really? Is it simply that jittery feeling you get before a big meeting, or is there more to it? That's what this chapter is all about.

Understanding what's going on behind the scenes is a total game-changer, which is why you need to dive into the nitty-gritty details of stress. The first thing you need to acknowledge is that stress affects you both mentally and physically. It's not just one or the other but a continuous cycle where these two elements influence each other. By peeking behind the scenes, you'll be able to understand what you're feeling physically and gain insight into why you're feeling that way.

So, what is stress? According to Hans Selye, who is known as the 'father of stress research', stress describes anything that seriously threatens the body's delicate balance, also known as homeostasis (Schneiderman et al., 2005). In other words, stress is anything that throws our system out of whack—whether it's a looming deadline, a surprise bill, or a never-ending to-do list. This means that stress is not just a mental game but also a physiological phenomenon. When you experience stress, your body triggers a complex interplay of hormones and bodily reactions, prepared to respond to the perceived danger. Let's break it down. Grab a seat and get ready to unravel the mysteries of stress.

Types of Stress

First things first, you need to know that stress isn't inherently bad. It's not the big, evil villain in every story you should be afraid of. That's because there are different types of stress, and sometimes, stress can be just what you need. Let's break down the different types of stress, starting with the short-term stuff, also known as *acute stress*.

Imagine this: You're sitting in a conference room, waiting for your turn to present a project to your colleagues. Your heart starts pounding, your palms get sweaty, and you feel like you might forget everything you've prepared. That's acute stress kicking in—a sudden surge of adrenaline and cortisol triggered by the pressure of the moment.

Acute stress is like a lightning bolt—it strikes fast and sharp but doesn't stick around for long. It's your body's natural response to a perceived threat or challenge, gearing you up for action and sharpening your focus. In situations like giving a presentation or facing a tight deadline, acute stress isn't just about sweaty palms and racing hearts. It can be your secret weapon, pushing you to perform at your peak and achieve your goals. How you perceive and respond to stressors can make all the difference. Instead of seeing it as a threat, try viewing acute stress as a signal that you're engaged, alert, and ready to take on the task at hand. With the right mindset, you can harness the energy of acute stress and turn it into a positive force for productivity and success.

Now, let's talk about its counterpart, *chronic stress*. This one's a bit trickier because it sticks around for the long haul. Chronic stress is like that unwanted houseguest who just won't leave—it lingers and lingers, wreaking havoc on our physical and mental health. It's the kind of stress that comes from ongoing issues like financial struggles, relationship troubles, or health problems. When stress becomes chronic, your body and mind are stuck in overdrive, unable to find relief. Chronic stress isn't just about feeling frazzled all the time. It can have serious long-term consequences for your health, from weakened immune systems to increased risk of heart disease and mental health disorders like anxiety and depression (Australian Psychological Society, 2022).

But here's the thing about chronic stress: It's not always about one big, catastrophic event. Sometimes, it's the accumulation of smaller stressors over time that wears you down. Think of it like a pile of bricks stacking up one by one. Individually, they might not seem like much, but put them all together, and suddenly, you're carrying a heavy load. That's why it's so important to recognize the signs of chronic stress and take steps to manage it before it takes a toll on your well-being.

So, whether you're dealing with a short-term stressor or wrestling with a chronic one, know that you're not alone. You'll explore strategies throughout this book to help you navigate the ups and downs of stress and emerge stronger and more resilient on the other side. To further understand what stress is, you need to explore its impact on your emotional and physical health, so let's take a look, starting with the emotional symptoms.

Emotional Symptoms of Stress

Ever find yourself with a pit in your stomach, your brain going into overdrive, and suddenly, you're spiraling out of control, thinking of all the worst-case scenarios and how this might just be the end of the world? Don't worry, we've all been there. When you experience stress, it affects you physically and emotionally. Emotionally, you might notice the following signs (Signs and Symptoms of Stress, 2022):

- All the patience leaves your body as you feel irritable, angry, and unable to enjoy activities.
- An overwhelming sense of burden, nervousness, and anxiety takes over your body as your racing thoughts prevent you from relaxing.
- Severe feelings of depression, mood swings, and a general loss of interest in life might creep up on you.
- Existing mental health issues might get aggravated, and in severe cases, thoughts of suicide might arise, causing even more stress.

Let's say you've got a looming deadline at work, and the pressure is mounting. Your mind starts racing, thinking of all the things that could go wrong. Maybe you start brainstorming ways to avoid disaster, even though it hasn't happened yet. Perhaps you find yourself zoning out, hoping the stress will magically disappear. But stress doesn't just mess with your head—it can also affect how you interact with those around you. Have you ever caught yourself snapping at a loved one for no apparent reason? Yes, that's stress rearing its ugly head.

Let's be real. Everyone knows they should handle stress better—for their own sake and for the people they care about. But sometimes, it feels like you're drowning in a sea of overwhelm with no life raft in sight. Feeling stressed is totally normal. In fact, it's hardwired into your biology as a survival mechanism. The problem arises when that stress response gets cranked up to eleven or when it's triggered more often than it should. Whether you're feeling overwhelmed, anxious, irritable, or simply exhausted, I want you to know that you're not alone. Stress can sneak up on anyone, and admitting when you're struggling is a brave thing to do.

Now that you have a better idea of the symptoms of stress, it's time to focus on the physiological responses.

Physiological Responses to Stress

Let's peek behind the curtain and see what's going on inside your body when stress comes knocking. It all starts with the amygdala, a small but mighty part of the brain. The amygdala is the bodyguard of your emotions, always on high alert for potential threats or dangers. As soon as it senses trouble, it sets off a chain reaction known as the fight, flight, or freeze response (Lewis, 2021).

Imagine for a moment you're walking down the street when a large dog comes running at you, teeth gnarled and ready to pounce. Immediately, your amygdala will signal the alarm for danger, barking orders to the rest of the body. If flight mode gets activated, you'll most likely run into the nearest store or jump on a bus to get away from the dog. If your body is in fight mode, you might roll up your sleeves and get ready to push the dog away from you. Alternatively, you might trigger the freeze response, which is exactly what it sounds like: You'll stand very still, too scared to move, hoping the dog will run past you.

When you're faced with danger, the amygdala will first scan the situation, using your different senses to assess the danger. Next, it will trigger the fight, flight, or freeze response by communicating the appropriate message to the hypothalamus, which acts as a control center for hormone regulation. The hypothalamus, in turn, activates the hypothalamic-pituitary-adrenal (HPA) axis, which is just a fancy word to describe the communication pathway between the hypothalamus, the pituitary gland, and the adrenal gland. Your body then releases different hormones to support the command sent by the brain.

Cortisol, often called the stress hormone, increases blood sugar levels to provide readily available energy. In other words, it gives you a little energy boost to overcome the issue at hand and pull an all-nighter to prep for the meeting you have to present first thing in the morning. Alongside cortisol, adrenaline is a hormone that acts more rapidly, causing increased heart rate, breathing rate, and blood pressure. It prepares the body for immediate physical action, like escaping danger.

As you can see, the amygdala plays a pretty important role. Nestled snugly in the limbic system, the emotional center of the brain, the amygdala runs the show when it comes to stress. Back in the day, when your ancestors were dodging saber-toothed tigers, the response of the amygdala literally saved lives. But do you still need it today? The answer is a resounding yes! You might have traded dodging predators on the savannah fields for looming deadlines, endless to-do lists, and rush-hour traffic, but you still need the amygdala to manage life's stress. However, you run into some issues when it's triggered too often.

When that stress response gets activated too often or unnecessarily, it can wreak havoc on your body and mind. You end up feeling exhausted, on edge, and unable to think clearly. Instead of relying on your rational brain to make decisions, you're stuck in emotional overdrive, constantly scanning for danger (Lewis, 2021). So, while it's important to recognize that your stress response is deeply ingrained in your biology, it's also crucial to acknowledge that your modern-day life doesn't always require a fight, flight, or freeze reaction. By understanding how your body reacts to stress, you can start to find healthier ways to manage it and reclaim your sense of calm and control, allowing the amygdala to take a vacation.

The amygdala isn't the only one working overtime when you're constantly stressed. Enter the parasympathetic nervous system, aka the body's built-in brake system. This system acts like a calming force, tapping the brakes to slow down your body's stress response and bring things back to baseline. In other words, when you're feeling stressed out, and your amygdala is going into overdrive, your parasympathetic nervous system will prompt you to take a deep breath, hit pause, and dial down the stress response.

The prefrontal cortex works in conjunction with the parasympathetic nervous system. Imagine the prefrontal cortex as the manager, delegating tasks and ensuring that all employees are working at their best pace. Located just behind your forehead, the prefrontal cortex has a knack for holding onto information from your current situation and past experiences, helping you make wise choices. When stress barges in, your senses shoot signals to both your prefrontal cortex and the amygdala—the brain's emergency hotline. But the amygdala is like Usain Bolt, reacting lightning-fast to danger, while the prefrontal cortex is like Thomas Edison, taking its sweet time to mull over the details first.

In other words, the prefrontal cortex earns its paycheck by reigning in the panicky amygdala as soon as you're out of immediate danger. Whether it's by convincing you that the meeting with your boss is an annual evaluation meeting, not due to a mistake you've made, or by helping you understand that it's your jacket hanging over the door and not a dark figure creeping up on you, it brings logical thinking to the party. In many ways, the prefrontal cortex is the voice of reason amid the chaos of stress.

But if that's the case, why are you still drowning in stress? There could be a few reasons for it. Perhaps your amygdala's on overdrive, or there's a glitch in communication between your brain buddies. Maybe your prefrontal cortex is on the fritz, or it's missing some crucial information from your past experiences. Perhaps your brain has turned one too many lemons into lemonade and is simply desperate for a break. But before you freak out, don't worry; there is light at the end of this tunnel.

Your brain's a champ at adapting, and thanks to something known as neuroplasticity, you can reroute your thought patterns, paving the way for a brain that's more chill and connected. We'll talk more about this in a moment, but for now, it's important to understand what's happening in your body on a physiological level when stressed, as it then becomes easier to visualize how stress management strategies and techniques can help. Take deep breathing, for example. By taking slow, deep breaths, you're activating your parasympathetic nervous system, sending a signal to your body that it's okay to relax and unwind.

Similarly, practices like mindfulness and progressive muscle relaxation work by shifting your focus away from stressors and onto the present moment. As you engage in these strategies, you're essentially hitting the brakes on your body's stress response, allowing your parasympathetic nervous system to take over and restore a sense of calm. So, the next time you feel stress creeping in, remember: It's just your amygdala doing its thing. Armed with the knowledge that your parasympathetic nervous system is there to help, you can use stress management strategies to pump the brakes and bring your body back into balance. It's all about understanding the science behind stress and empowering yourself to take control of your body's stress response.

Focused Mode vs. Default Mode

Speaking of the body's stress response and how it occurs in the brain, let's examine the different modes it manifests in your day-to-day thinking. The two modes you need to be aware of are focused mode and default mode. Take a moment to imagine working on your dream project at work. You and your team are working like a well-oiled machine, and the project looks better than ever. Worries fade away as you and the team work hard while enjoying inside jokes. You don't even notice the time flying by as you're totally immersed and engaged in the fun of the project, feeling high on productivity and fulfillment. This is what is referred to as focused mode.

When you're in focused mode, your brain actively taps into a network of neurons known as the task-positive network. This can occur outside of work as well. Whether you're fully engaged in a conversation, focused on decorating the perfect cake, or immersed in your brush strokes as you're painting a canvas, focused mode can be activated. When you're in focused mode, worries fade away, and you're able to experience the mundane as extraordinary. You can also turn focused mode inward, allowing you to think deeply and solve problems creatively.

On the other end of the stick, you have default mode, which occurs when you are not fully present in the moment. You might be doing one thing while your mind is busy with something else. Say you're watching a movie, but while you're shoving the popcorn in your mouth, you're actually thinking about the kitchen renovation and your child who is down with the flu. Just like an idle engine, your thoughts are still consuming fuel, as if you're not resting at all. It's almost like your brain is still on guard, prepared to jump into action at any given point. The result? You never switch to focused mode.

As it turns out, your brain needs to deactivate this default mode network to perform tasks accurately. Imagine an athlete who barely slept the night before and felt too anxious to eat a healthy breakfast, about to sprint a 100-meter race. He gets down into the blocks and waits for the signal. As he waits, he grows anxious, not feeling as rested as the athlete next to him who had a good meal, proper sleep, and a protein shake. When you're not actively engaging with the world around you, your brain will likely do something else to keep busy. For example, if you're not engaging in the conversation around the dinner table, your brain will begin to run through tomorrow's to-do list, causing you to feel uneasy.

Your brain needs to switch from default mode to focused mode to manage stress, and that's what this book is all about. The strategies in this book are designed to help you do this, allowing you to deal with negative and anxious thoughts in a healthy and productive manner. When you're in default mode, your brain is often dealing with thoughts like these, which can amplify feelings of stress. But when you shift to focused mode, you're more engaged and present, reducing those stress levels significantly.

For example, mindfulness exercises, one of the techniques this book will discuss, will help bring your attention to the present moment. This practice engages your prefrontal cortex—the part of your brain responsible for rational thinking and problem-solving. When your prefrontal cortex is active, it allows you to enter focused mode and resist stress. Your goal is to increase the time you spend in focused mode, wield greater influence over your spontaneous thoughts, and eventually change your inner dialogue. By doing this, you can effortlessly cultivate positive thoughts. This doesn't mean you'll never slip into default mode—it's a natural and necessary part of how your brain works. But with practice, you can increase your ability to switch back to focused mode when needed, reducing stress's impact and improving your overall well-being.

Spending more time in focused mode means being more present and engaged with the world around you and your tasks at hand. This state allows you to push past the automatic negative thinking patterns that often crop up during times of stress. By actively choosing to redirect your thoughts and attention, you can begin to reshape your inner dialogue. Instead of the constant chatter of self-doubt, worry, and rumination, your mind can become filled with encouragement, optimism, and problem-solving insights.

Your Instinctive Focus

Understanding how your instinctive focus works is essential to managing stress effectively and redirecting your attention towards more positive and productive thoughts. But what is it? Have you ever noticed how your attention seems to be drawn to certain things, almost like a magnet pulling you in? There's a reason for that, and according to Amit Sood, it's called instinctive focus (Sood, 2013).

Your brain is wired to prioritize information that falls into one of three categories: threat, pleasure, and novelty. It's like your brain has a built-in radar, constantly scanning your surroundings for anything that could be a danger, a source of pleasure, or something new and exciting. But your brain tends to gravitate toward negativity, known as the negativity bias. Your mind is more attuned to threats and dangers than to positive experiences. While being on high alert might have served your ancestors well in the wild, it can wreak havoc on your mental well-being in today's world.

Take a moment to think about it: How often do you find yourself getting caught up in negative thoughts and worries while positive experiences pass by unnoticed? It's like your mind is constantly restless, searching for something to latch onto, even if it's something that brings you down. Surprisingly, your mind is ignorant when it comes to predicting what will make you happy. People often spend more time imagining future pleasure than actually experiencing joy in the present moment. Sadly, this often results in chasing after happiness and never fully appreciating the here and now.

But here's the silver lining: Your brain is also wired to be drawn to novelty. When something is new and unfamiliar, your mind lights up with curiosity and excitement, fully engaged in the present moment. It's like your brain's way of saying, "Hey, pay attention! This is something different and interesting." So, if you find yourself getting caught up in negative thoughts or worries, know that it's completely normal. Your brain is wired to focus on the negative, but that doesn't mean you're stuck with it.

The chapters ahead will explore techniques to shift your focus away from negativity and toward the present moment. You'll learn how to cultivate gratitude, savor positive experiences, and find joy in the here and now. While your instinctive focus may sometimes lead you astray, you have the power to train your mind to focus on the good stuff.

Stress and Neuroplasticity

As I just mentioned, you have the power to retrain your mind to focus on good things instead of always seeking danger. Your brain has the ability to change and adapt, which is a process known as neuroplasticity. Think of it as a light switch that you can rewire to work differently than before. You can, in a sense, rewire your brain to respond to stress in a more positive way. There is also no age limit to brain rewiring. No matter your age, you can always teach your brain a few new tricks. As long as you're still willing to learn, you can tap into the functions of neuroplasticity.

Have you ever seen someone create glasswork? Blowing glass is this incredible art form where you start with solid materials, add heat and air, and create a shapeable material. Brains are a bit like that. You might think something is set in stone, but with the right tools and skills, you can reshape your brain and allow new cells and neurons to form. Similar to glassblowing, your brain can connect positive actions to certain prompts by gluing them together, metaphorically speaking. In other words, you can retrain your brain to respond to stress in a way that is helpful instead of sending you into a downward spiral.

Neuroplasticity isn't just about learning new things but also about remaining flexible and adaptable, which is a crucial skill to have if you want to survive in this modern chaos of today. By being adaptable and flexible, you'd be able to adjust when life throws a spanner in the works instead of falling apart and assuming the worst. Rewiring your brain will require hard work, but it will be worth it. The work you put in today will determine the quality of your tomorrow, so let that motivate you to get started.

The brain is incredibly powerful, so don't sell yourself short by assuming that you can't change or you'll never overcome stress. Tap into the power of the mind, knowing that it's an unstoppable tool with so much potential. All the stress and worries running through your mind are only cluttering your brain's capacity to focus. Imagine driving in a car in the middle of traffic. Now, add a screaming baby in the back seat, a radio on full blast, and a cell phone that won't stop ringing. It's a nightmare, right? That's what's happening in your mind when you're constantly worried and stressed. But with neuroplasticity, you can turn down the radio, lull the baby back to sleep, and put the phone on silent, allowing you to focus more effectively.

Stress can steal your daily joy, but you have the power to reclaim it. You can redirect your thought processes, build more present-focused and hopeful neural pathways, and create a more interconnected, smoothly functioning brain. In essence, by understanding and harnessing the power of neuroplasticity, you can transform how your brain responds to stress. You can train your brain to view life stressors as manageable challenges rather than insurmountable threats. It's all about building those positive, productive brain pathways and enlarging the parts of your brain that help you think clearly.

So, here's to a future where you're not just surviving stress but thriving despite it. With the right mindset and tools, you can rewire your brain for resilience, joy, and success. The exercises and practices outlined in this book are designed to help calm down your brain's automatic stress response, making stressors seem more manageable and less overwhelming. By incorporating these strategies into your daily life, you can train your brain to respond to stress in a healthier, more adaptive way.

While this chapter has covered the intricate workings of stress and its impact on your mind and body, it is only the beginning. Up next, let's explore the causes of stress and dive deeper into understanding it.

2

WHAT ARE THE CAUSES OF STRESS?

HAVE you ever stopped to ask yourself *why* you are stressed? I've been in so many conversations where I'm quick to say, "It's going good; I'm just stressed," without giving the cause of the stress a second thought. "What do you mean *why* am I stressed?" I'm stressed because I'm stressed, right? Actually, that's not a reason. Feeling stressed is the symptom of something else that's going on, and if you want to overcome stress, you need to dig a little deeper and identify the cause of it.

The more you understand the triggers behind your stress, the more power you have to make meaningful changes. Identifying the specific circumstances, thoughts, or behaviors that lead to stress allows you to address them head-on. By examining your stress closely, you can develop targeted strategies to reduce or eliminate it. Without this deep understanding, you may find yourself applying generic solutions that only scratch the surface of your stress, leaving you feeling overwhelmed and powerless. The key to breaking free from the cycle of stress lies in unraveling its roots and tackling them at the source.

So, where do you begin? First, you need to become aware that there are different types of stress. As mentioned in the previous chapter, not all stress is bad, but most people have been affected by bad stress. To understand the cause of your stress, you need to differentiate between everyday stress, major stress, and traumatic stress. Let's start with the most common one and explore the everyday causes of stress.

Everyday Causes of Stress

Everyday causes of stress can be categorized into two groups. On the one hand, you have the daily hassles. You know, traffic jams, misplacing your keys, spam callers trying to sell you another insurance you don't need—that sort of thing. On the other hand, you have chronic stressors, which are the more significant, persistent issues that linger in the background of your daily life, like financial struggles or a teenager who is acting up. But both hassles and chronic stressors are consistent in your daily life, like a tiny pebble that has found its way into your shoe, not so much of a big deal that you stop walking, but enough to cause constant discomfort.

These daily causes of stress can add up and eventually trigger a pretty serious stress response from your amygdala. It might not be serious enough for you to want to take action immediately, but it will continuously put pressure on your mental and physical well-being, as discussed in Chapter 1. That's why you shouldn't overlook everyday causes of stress or shrug it off as "not so bad." There's a reason so many people are overwhelmed and stressed, and it's not necessarily due to something huge; it's often these everyday causes that are adding up.

To identify daily stressors in your life, you need to have a clear picture of what hassles and chronic stressors might look like to the average Joe. Like weeds in a garden, daily hassles tend to keep popping back up, no matter how many times you cut them down.

Does that mean it's a hopeless case? Of course not. It simply means that you might have to adjust your approach.

Here's an example: A good friend of mine is a bit of a neat freak. She wants her house to be spotless at all times. Have you tried keeping your home spotless with two children and a husband who doesn't use a coaster? It's almost impossible. For her, a dirty kitchen is a daily stressor. It's something she experiences every day, and while it's nothing major, it bothers her constantly. This then leads to feeling agitated and irritated with the rest of her family.

My friend has two options: be annoyed with her family for using another clean glass right after she cleaned the kitchen, or adjust her approach. Instead of seeing a kitchen with used dishes as "dirty," she can begin to rewire her brain and see it as a kitchen where a loving family just shared a warm meal, changing it to something positive. Instead of chasing perfection, she can set up a cleaning schedule, knowing that the kitchen will be cleaned, just not at all times of the day.

Take a moment to think of the hassles in your life. Can you begin to notice that, with a rewired mind, as discussed in Chapter 1, you can eliminate them as stressors? Remember, these hassles are like background noise that creates the soundtrack to your life, causing tension and anxiety. They can seep into every corner of your being and drain your energy and resilience.

Now, let's focus on the chronic stressors. Can you remember what was said about chronic stress in the first chapter? Even though not all stress is bad, chronic stress falls into that category because it sends your body into overdrive. Chronic stressors seem to get your attention more effectively than hassles, but they can also make you feel hopeless. When you deal with the same stressor day after day, you might start wondering if there is a way out. Take, for example, dealing with an overbearing mother-in-law who shows up to your home unannounced daily to assess your skills as a spouse or aiding a family member who is battling an illness, their pain constantly an ache in your heart as you cater to their daily needs. These things happen daily, and they're not just small annoyances but heavy things to carry both physically and emotionally.

This includes that boss of yours who seems to thrive on making your life miserable, turning every workday into a minefield of stress and frustration. Whether it's the micromanaging boss breathing down your neck or the passive-aggressive colleague determined to undermine you, workplace relationships can be a significant source of stress. Paired with long hours, you might end up feeling like you're running a marathon, and right as the finish line is in sight, you have to do it all again.

One thing is clear: You shouldn't underestimate the severity of daily stressors in your life. Instead of claiming that it's simply "part of life," you should evaluate your daily stressors and determine ways to either eliminate them from your life completely or find a way to think about them more positively. When your brain is constantly dealing with hassles and chronic stressors, your poor amygdala will never catch a break, making it even harder for your brain to switch off and relax.

Major Causes of Stress

Have you ever had an experience and knew, "Wow, my life will never be the same again?" I'm not talking about discovering mocha-flavored ice cream for the first time. I'm talking about big things, like buying a house, losing a job, or seeing that positive line on the pregnancy test. These are the types of things that cause significant stress in your life. There are different types of major stress, such as developmental transitions, happy causes, and bad causes. To understand the major causes of stress in your life, you need to understand these different types and begin to notice if they are present.

Major life transitions can feel like being tossed into a stormy sea without a life jacket. It's that classic pre-birth freak out or significant doubt as you're about to get on that plane to start a new life somewhere else. Whether major events are positive or negative, they can stir up a whirlwind of emotions. This might come as a surprise to you, but even some of the best moments in your life can cause subconscious stress. In fact, that's one of the reasons I started my research into stress.

I always thought my most major stressful event would be something negative, like losing my job. But as it turns out, my most major stressful event to date was my wedding and moving to a new country. Don't get me wrong, I was beyond excited to embark on this new adventure and chapter of my life, and I didn't even think I was stressed. Yet, my body acted otherwise, and a few months before my big move to Australia, I started getting the most intense migraines of my life. As a bonus, my skin also started breaking out, which is every bride's dream. Am I right? As a result, I was incredibly anxious and irritable, and in full transparency, not a very pleasant person to be around.

The developmental transitions of life are considered some of the most significant causes of stress, even when they are exciting. Developmental transitions are pivotal moments that force you to adapt to new circumstances. This includes everything from starting college to becoming a parent. These transitions can be even trickier and more anxiety-inducing when they are out of your control or when it's not your own decision, like being kicked out of your apartment because the landlord wants to sell the building or being forced to move out of your childhood home because your parents are downsizing to a smaller house. These changes can feel like a tidal wave pulling you under.

Similarly, happy changes can be equally stressful and change your life forever. When you put in an offer for your dream home, it's exhilarating, but it's also nerve-wracking. Suddenly, there are a million decisions to make, and the pressure is on to make everything work, especially as you dip deeply into your savings account for the down payment. This is good stress, which comes from positive experiences. While it fuels you to push forward and grow, it can also be temporarily negative for your body, especially when the stress lingers for a prolonged time.

The *Mayo Clinic Guide to Stress-Free Living* talks about different flavors of stress, categorizing them as good, bad, or ugly (Sood, 2013). Good stress was already covered, so what is bad or ugly stress? Bad stress creeps into your life when demands exceed your coping abilities. Like an overworked schedule or a mountain of responsibilities for which you don't have time. Bad stress can turn the once enjoyable moments into a source of anxiety and exhaustion, which often happens in the workplace. But before you lose hope and feel tempted to quit your job, you can turn bad stress into good stress. With the right tools and strategies, such as those in this book, you can change your perception of the stressor into something good. An example of this would be viewing rejection as an opportunity to grow instead of a setback in life.

Significant causes of stress can also lead to what's called ugly stress. That's the kind of stress that comes from facing life's most challenging moments. In other words, ugly stress is bad stress multiplied by ten. Suppose someone is diagnosed with a chronic condition. Their days are filled with pain, fatigue, and uncertainty about the future. However, even ugly stress can be turned into good stress with the right tools and mindset. For example, amid the turmoil, they might find meaning, which would provide them with the strength to face each day.

In essence, major causes of stress aren't only about the events themselves; it's about how you perceive and respond to them. So, whether it's navigating a major life transition or dealing with illness, it's important to recognize the impact that these events can have on your life. By understanding the difference between good and bad stress and learning how to cope with the challenges that come your way, you can deal with these major causes of stress with resilience and grace.

Realizing that my body was reacting to what I perceived as positive events was a wake-up call. It made me question how stress manifests itself and how our bodies respond, even to situations we believe we're handling well. My story became a catalyst for diving into stress management strategies and understanding the complex interplay between our mind and body. By putting the strategies in this book into action, I learned to better cope with life's challenges and cultivate resilience in the face of adversity. My experiences taught me that stress is inevitable, but how you respond to it is within your control.

Traumatic Causes of Stress

As you might know, traumatic causes of stress can have a profound impact on your life, affecting not only your emotional well-being but also your physical health. While many associate trauma with extreme events like combat or natural disasters, it can also stem from core experiences, especially during childhood. Let's take a closer look by exploring what trauma really is.

In short, trauma refers to any event that poses a threat to your life or physical well-being or to the lives of those you care about. This includes experiences like physical or sexual abuse, neglect, witnessing violence, or even a serious illness or injury. While not everyone who experiences trauma develops post-traumatic stress disorder (PTSD), it can still have lasting effects on your mental and physical health, and you may experience symptoms such as vivid flashbacks, intrusive thoughts, nightmares, trembling, and being upset easily.

Traumatic causes of stress also include Adverse Childhood Experiences (ACEs), which refer to stressful or traumatic events that occur during childhood. These types of traumatic causes of stress can have long-lasting effects and can continue well into adulthood. ACEs include things like physical, emotional, or sexual abuse, neglect, or growing up in a household with substance abuse or mental illness. Trauma and ACEs can change the way your brain responds to stress. As a quick reminder, the amygdala is what triggers the fight, flight, or freeze response, and it sends signals to the rest of your body to prepare for danger. At the same time, the prefrontal cortex acts as the brake, helping you to calm down and think rationally in stressful situations.

When you experience trauma or chronic stress, especially during childhood development, the amygdala can become hyperactive. This means it's more likely to perceive threats, even when they're not present. Trauma and ACEs can also weaken the prefrontal cortex's ability to regulate the amygdala, which can lead to a stress response that is difficult to control. In other words, ACEs make you more sensitive to everyday stressors, causing you to react more strongly or feel overwhelmed more easily. This can manifest as symptoms like anxiety, anger, difficulty concentrating, or even physical health issues like chronic pain or heart disease. So, when you've experienced trauma or ACEs, there can be a bit of a tug-of-war between your amygdala and your prefrontal cortex. Your amygdala might be sounding the alarm bells, telling you to panic or flee, while your prefrontal cortex struggles to calm things down and think logically.

If you've experienced trauma or ACEs, it's essential to acknowledge that it can affect your stress response. You might find yourself feeling on edge or anxious in situations that others find manageable. And that's okay. It's not your fault, and you're not alone. Seeking therapy or professional help can be incredibly beneficial in processing trauma and learning healthy coping mechanisms. Alongside therapy and professional guidance, the strategies and techniques outlined in this book can also play a role in managing stress. By learning to regulate your stress response and develop resilience, you can begin to take control of your well-being and navigate life's challenges more effectively.

From everyday stressors to significant life transitions and even traumatic experiences, it's clear that stress comes in all shapes and sizes. But you're not alone in dealing with stress. Whether it's good stress pushing you forward or bad stress weighing you down, there are ways to manage it. Remember, your brain is a powerful tool, and with the right strategies, you can train it to handle stress more effectively. The next chapter will continue to inspect the foundations of stress and explore its consequences.

3

WHAT ARE THE CONSEQUENCES OF STRESS?

HAVE you ever paused for a moment to think about what would happen if you didn't manage your stress? Would it really be that bad? Are the consequences *that* severe, or have you made it worse in your mind than in reality? Now, before you start stressing about your stress, take a deep breath and know that the intention of this chapter isn't to scare you but to motivate you to take action.

Knowing that stress is bad for you from a general point of view is like knowing takeout food isn't the healthiest choice: you're aware of it, but you probably don't care that much that you'll stop eating takeout altogether. You might know that stress is affecting you but not recognize the extent of its consequences. This chapter will delve into truly understanding what stress is doing to your mind and body.

If you feel an added heap of stress because you know stress is affecting you, I totally understand, but don't fear. As soon as I've discussed the consequences, I'll jump into how you can get started on your stress-relieving journey.

Since there are different types of stress, it comes as no surprise that acute and chronic stress affect you differently. Let's start by exploring the consequences of acute stress on your mind and body.

The Consequences of Acute Stress

Chapter 1 described acute stress as your body's initial response to a threat or challenge, allowing you to gear up for action and sharpen your focus. It's neither inherently bad nor good but a natural process of what you perceive as danger. But what are the effects of acute stress on the body? Are sweaty palms and a trembling voice all there is to it? Unfortunately not. Acute stress can affect you in various ways, including cognitively, emotionally, physically, and behaviorally.

Cognitively, stress can manifest as constant worrying. When you spend more time worrying about what might happen or what has already happened rather than being in the present moment, it's a sign that you are experiencing acute stress. Acute stress can also affect your cognitive health by causing racing thoughts and the inability to focus. Have you ever been so stressed that even the simplest question seems hard? That's what acute stress can do to you. It can also cause you to focus more on the negatives, encouraging you to adopt a pessimistic view of life (Marks, 2023).

The emotional symptoms or effects of acute stress are more subtle, and people often miss these signs of stress. It includes feeling agitated, moody, and frustrated, as well as easily becoming overwhelmed with mundane tasks. One of the most prominent effects of acute stress on your emotional well-being is that you will struggle to relax and quiet your mind, finding something to stress about even when you're on a sandy beach enjoying a cocktail. Another emotional symptom of acute stress is feeling bad about yourself and having very low self-esteem. This might not seem related to stress at first, but it's a clear sign that it's time to take action (Mayo Clinic, 2023).

The physical symptoms of acute stress are the most common signs, and while it includes sweaty palms, there is more to it. Physical symptoms of acute stress can include low energy, headaches, an upset stomach, and even insomnia. Acute stress can lower your sexual desire and cause jaw pain due to clenching and grinding your teeth. Some physical symptoms that not many people are aware of are aches, pains, and tense muscles, along with ringing in the ears and chest pain (Marks, 2023). In other words, it's more than just a nervous shaking hand and should be taken seriously.

Finally, acute stress can affect your behavior. This is one of the consequences that is quite hard to notice in yourself but easy to spot in those you know well. Acute stress can cause a change in your appetite, where you either start eating more or less than you are used to. It can also make you procrastinate more and avoid responsibilities, even when you are known as someone responsible. Unfortunately, acute stress can also lead to an increase in alcohol and drug usage, and while it might feel like it's managing the stress in the moment, it will only prolong the effects and can even worsen it. Another way that acute stress can affect your behavior is by having more nervous behaviors such as nail biting, fidgeting, and pacing (Marks, 2023).

Acute stress is often overlooked, as you might not recognize just how damaging it can be to your life. While you've now looked at how it can affect you cognitively, physically, emotionally, and behaviorally, there is another major consequence of stress, and that is the effect it can have on your relationships.

Acute Stress and Relationships

When you're stressed, you tend to be more irritable, among many other things, so it's natural that it might cause a few hiccups in your relationships. Stress doesn't only affect romantic relationships but also the relationships you have with friends, family, and even coworkers. Imagine being stressed at work because you're pressed for time preparing for an important meeting, and then your coworker comes into your office just to have a chat. Super stressed and anxious, you tell them to leave you alone and to work on their own project.

However, due to the stress, you communicate it slightly passive-aggressively and immediately feel the tension between you and your coworker. Yikes!

That's just one example of how stress can damper relationships. When you snap at your partner or friend, they'll most likely get upset and snap back, creating a loop. It's like a negative cycle where you end up "catching" each other's stress, and before you know it, you're in the middle of a heated argument that came out of nowhere (Lau et al., 2019).

To put it bluntly, stress doesn't discriminate. It affects everyone, and it definitely doesn't play nicely with people's closest bonds. When stress creeps in, it can mess with you emotionally and physically, which, in turn, changes how you behave around your partner. Because, let's face it, you're super comfy around them, so you might not even realize when stress starts to rear its head in your relationship. However, when you notice the stress in the relationship, you can do something about it before it's too late. Here are a few signs that stress might be affecting your relationships:

- You have no desire for sexual intimacy within a romantic relationship and find it hard to connect with one another.
- You sweat the small stuff, like getting upset with your partner over the direction of the spoons in the cutlery drawer or having a go at your coworkers over who opened the window in the break room at work.
- You constantly feel under attack and look for ways to outsmart your friends or family in conversation.
- You feel a sudden lack of trust and feel betrayed for no apparent reason.
- Things that used to attract you to your partner are suddenly a huge turnoff.

- You feel the urge to escape from everyone and live alone in a small mountain cabin.

These are just a few ways stress can worm its way into your relationships, but they're some of the most common. So, if any of these sound familiar, it might be time to step back and address the stress before it does any more damage. Here's the million-dollar question: how much relationship stress is too much?

Surprisingly, a little bit of tension here and there is totally normal and can be good for the relationship. But if you're finding yourselves stuck in a cycle of misunderstandings, communication breakdowns, or unmet expectations, it might be time to reassess and find the cause of all the drama. Pay attention to how often you're feeling unhappy or disappointed in your relationship, and don't be afraid to address any red flags head-on. After all, a healthy relationship is all about weathering the storm together, not getting swept away by it. Just like personal stress, relationship stress can be managed.

When you look at stress in the right way, it can improve the relationship and not harm it. Instead of seeing stress as this huge monster you must fight alone, you can see it as an opportunity to open up and support each other. When you share your stress with your loved ones and they respond with love and understanding, you and your loved ones have the opportunity to build a super strong bond that can handle anything life throws your way. To manage stress effectively, you should talk about what's stressing you out and what you need from each other when you're feeling overwhelmed.

It might be tough to open up about what's bothering you at first, especially if it's something within the relationship itself, but it's worth it. The couples and friendships who thrive are the ones who tackle stress as a team. They stick together through thick and thin, and that feeling of being in it together is priceless. The same goes for your team at work or any other group you might be part of. You'll feel a sense of relief when you share your stress with others.

The Consequences of Chronic Stress

Now that you understand the consequences of acute stress, it's time to focus on the other type of stress introduced in Chapter 1: chronic stress. Chronic stress can wreak havoc both physically and mentally. It's not a silly little thing that will pass by itself but something that should be taken seriously, as it can impact many aspects of your life, including your brain, heart health, weight management, immune system, and cellular aging. I know it sounds scary, but the fact that you're here, reading this book, means that you've already taken an essential step toward a healthier, peaceful future. The best way to assess the consequences of chronic stress is by exploring the different areas it affects individually, starting with the brain.

Stress and Your Brain

Have you ever watched one of those robotic vacuum cleaners run out of battery? It's quite comical and slightly sad to watch the little robot start moving slower and slower, passing by heaps of dust without noticing it, desperately trying to do a good job but simply not having the power to do so. That's a great representation of what stress does to the brain. When stress becomes a long-term companion, it throws your brain's groove out of whack. Your brain cells struggle to grab the energy they need, leaving them vulnerable to damage and a little confused. The excess cortisol (the stress hormone released when you're experiencing a stressful situation) acts like a wrecking ball for your hippocampus—the part of your brain responsible for learning, memory, and mood.

Chronic stress affects your brain in more than one way. Over a longer period of time, it can hardwire your brain to get stuck in a constant "emergency mode," making it tough for the logical part of your brain to calm down your stress response (Greenberg, 2017). In other words, you'll be on high alert all the time, and even the smallest stressor will feel like a huge task.

Let's take a closer look at how chronic stress affects the brain.

- **Chronic stress increases mental illness:** Researchers have uncovered that chronic stress is a significant player in the development of various psychiatric conditions like depression, bipolar disorder, and post-traumatic stress disorder (Davis et al., 2017). Studies suggest that chronic stress can lead to lasting changes in the brain's structure, possibly explaining why those enduring chronic stress are more susceptible to mood and anxiety disorders later in life. For instance, one study found that chronic stress can result in more myelin-producing cells but fewer neurons, disrupting brain communication and negatively impacting the hippocampus (Chetty et al., 2014). Why is that concerning? Because your hippocampus is in charge of your memory, specifically partial memory, memory consolidation, and memory transfer. When the hippocampus isn't running at its best capacity, you will be more forgetful, struggle to recall even the most basic things, and even forget things that are important to you.
- **Stress kills brain cells:** Not only does chronic stress mess with your brain's structure, but it can also destroy your brain cells. The hormones released during stress can target and destroy neurons, particularly the newly formed ones. Chronic stress can even put the brakes on the production of new neurons in the hippocampus— the brain region crucial for memory and emotion (Yaribeygi et al., 2017). The excessive stress and cortisol overload can also ramp up the production of glutamate, a neurotransmitter linked to mood regulation and cognition. Too much glutamate? It can spell trouble,

contributing to neurodegenerative diseases like Alzheimer's and Parkinson's (Pal, 2021).
- **Stress shrinks the brain:** Stress doesn't stop at impeding brain cell development; it can also shrink your brain volume. Even in seemingly healthy individuals, constant exposure to high cortisol levels can shrink brain areas vital for regulating emotions, metabolism, and memory (Cherry, 2019). High cortisol levels have been associated with greater brain volume loss and poorer cognitive performance on memory tests. And it's not just major stressors that can wreak havoc; everyday stressors can pile up over time, reducing resilience to future stress (Ansell et al., 2012).
- **Stress hurts your memory:** Have you ever noticed that stressful events can make it challenging to recall details? That's because stress can throw a spanner in your memory works. Even minor stress can mess with your memory, like forgetting where you put your keys when you're rushing out the door. Animal studies have shown that chronic stress can impair spatial memory and short-term memory, particularly in older subjects (Hyer et al., 2023). While a little stress before a big event might give your memory a boost, too much stress, especially when trying to learn something, can sabotage your recall abilities. It's all about finding that stress sweet spot for memory enhancement without the memory meltdown.

Stress and Your Heart

The second aspect of your health that chronic stress impacts is your heart health, and considering that heart health is one of the major reasons for death in America, this shouldn't be taken lightly. When you experience stress on a daily basis, your heart gets bombarded with stress hormones, which can be a serious hazard to your well-being. Chronic stress can chip away at your heart health by negatively affecting the lining of your blood vessels, which elevates the risk of hypertension, stroke, and heart attack (Greenberg, 2017).

This isn't new information, though; scientists have been working hard to connect stress and heart diseases. In a 2021 study involving 118,706 people without pre-existing heart disease across 21 countries, researchers discovered that high stress was linked to an increased risk of cardiovascular disease, coronary heart disease, stroke, and even death (Santosa et al., 2021). The American Heart Association found that the accumulation of everyday stresses could heighten the risk of cardiovascular disease due to perceived stress and work-related stress (Levine et al., 2021).

Physiologically, stress causes heightened activity in the amygdala, which increases the production of white blood cells in bone marrow, leading to inflammation in the arteries. Why does that matter? Because inflammation raises the risk of cardiovascular events such as chest pain, heart attacks, and strokes (Tawakol et al., 2017). In other words, chronic stress can be hard on your heart and it can add a lot of extra pressure on your body to function effectively.

Stress and Weight Gain

You now know that stress affects the brain and the heart, but did you know it can also affect your weight? As discussed in previous chapters, chronic stress elevates your cortisol levels, known as the stress hormone. In immediate stressful situations, cortisol helps you to get out of it, but when you have high levels of cortisol for an extended period, it starts to become a problem for your weight. Why? Because cortisol also happens to be a major appetite booster (Lindberg, 2019).

When stress becomes the norm, it's no wonder you find yourself reaching for those comforting snacks. All the additional snacks and comforting foods add to the excess calories consumed during the day, which tend to settle around the midsection. How rude of it, am I right? To add insult to injury, a 2015 study revealed that stress can throw your metabolism off track as well. Researchers found that women who reported feeling stressed burned 104 fewer calories after eating a high-fat meal than non-stressed women. To put it into perspective, that's like gaining almost 11 pounds in a year (Kiecolt-Glaser et al., 2015). On top of slowing down your metabolism, chronic stress also causes higher insulin levels, which can be dangerous in itself and lead to diabetes.

Stress and Your Immune System

Do you ever feel like you're constantly sick? Like you just can't escape the endless cycle of one cold after the other, only with a brief moment of relief in between? There might be a reason for it, and no, it's not because the universe hates you. According to research, chronic stress weakens your immune system and leaves you more susceptible to infection and inflammation. In other words, when stress overstays its welcome, your body's defense system pays the price (Cleveland Clinic, 2017).

Due to the high cortisol production when you're chronically stressed, your body eventually gets accustomed to the stress, which paves the way for more inflammation. In other words, you'll continue to get sick, and when you're sick, it will increase your chances of getting even worse. On top of that, chronic stress puts a damper on your body's lymphocytes—the white blood cells that play a crucial role in fending off infections. With fewer lymphocytes, you become more vulnerable to viruses like the common cold and cold sores. It's like your immune system starts waving a white flag, unable to put up a strong defense against illnesses (Cleveland Clinic, 2017).

Over time, the chronic stress leaves your immune system overworked, exhausted, and unable to protect you from diseases. Unfortunately, this opens the door for various immune-related diseases to shoot their shot, including arthritis, fibromyalgia, lupus, psoriasis, and inflammatory bowel disease (Pietrangelo, 2017).

Stress and Cellular Aging

The final consequence of chronic stress that you should be aware of is cellular aging. This is where things get really wild. Chronic stress can speed up the aging process at a cellular level. Yes, you read that right. Researchers found that moms under chronic stress had shorter telomeres—the protective caps on DNA—equivalent to a whopping 10 years of extra aging (Greenberg, 2017). In other words, stress can quite literally age you biologically. You have your real age, determined by the year you were born, and a cellular age, which is the age your body is equal to. With a lot of stress, your body can feel 40 when you're 30. That's why finding ways to manage your stress and lighten the mental load is essential.

Now that you've seen how stress can wreak havoc on your mind and body, it's time to take the reins and regain control. The next few chapters will explore strategies that empower you to tackle stress head-on and shift your mindset for the better. Stress may be a part of life, but it doesn't have to dictate your well-being. Reclaim your peace of mind and build a healthier, happier future—one stress-busting strategy at a time.

4

STRESS-RELIEF BREATHING

THE PREVIOUS THREE chapters created a strong foundation by diving into the basics of stress. Now that you have a clear understanding of what stress is, how it's caused, and the consequences it can have on your life, it's time to embrace the S-I-M-P-L-E framework strategies that will help you regain control. The first strategy is stress-relief breathing, also known as breathwork.

When you're stressed, your breath is the first to react. Have you ever noticed how out of breath you feel when you're presenting at work or answering questions on a blind date? You might have thought the stairs were to blame, but it's actually your body's first stress response. That's why we'll dive into the wonderful world of breathwork first and how it can be a game-changer when dealing with stress.

This chapter will explore various breathing techniques that can aid in calming your mind and body, even when everything feels chaotic. It will also examine how you can use breathwork in your daily life. So, get ready to inhale peace and exhale all the bad vibes.

Introduction to Breathwork

When stress hits, you're first presented with physical symptoms, such as an increased heart rate and shallow breathing, which then leads to negative self-talk and other mental symptoms. But what if you could stop stress before it got to that? What if you could catch it when it first appears, stopping it right in its tracks? That's the beauty of breathwork.

Stress takes you through different stages, and breathwork focuses on gaining control of your breathing to prevent stress from going any further. By gaining control of your breathing, you'll be able to remain calm and assess the situation without spiraling out of control. Both gaining control of your breathing and remaining calm are part of mindfulness, which will be discussed in great detail later on. For now, all you need to know is that breathwork can be an essential first line of defense against stress that spins out of control.

When done consistently, breathwork can have incredible long-term advantages, such as pain reduction, but that doesn't mean it's not helpful immediately as well. For example, say you're going about your day when, suddenly, stress hits. Your heart starts racing, and you're breathing faster than a sprinter at the finish line. Your mind begins to spiral, but you decide to take a couple of minutes and practice breathwork. Before you know it, your heart rate slows down, you feel calmer, and those ruminating thoughts are something of the past. Doesn't that sound pretty amazing? Let's take a moment to explore exactly how these breathwork techniques work and why they are effective.

How Breathwork Helps

Take a moment to imagine this: You're chilling at home, snuggled on the couch, watching your favorite show, when, suddenly, there's a mysterious noise in the back garden. You know it's probably just the neighbor's cat or that storm you saw on the news coming in, but your brain jumps into full alert mode. Your sympathetic nervous system gets activated, and before you know it, your heart is racing like you're at the gym, and your breath is in overdrive. Wishing you had never watched all those scary movies as a teen, your mind is telling you to hide in the closet or, if you're braver than me, grab the baseball bat and investigate.

Now, here's the thing: Your brain doesn't always get it right. Sometimes, it sees stressors where there aren't any, based on past experiences or simply because it's having a particularly jumpy day. Once you see the cat on the back porch, minding its business, your parasympathetic nervous system can bring back the calm after the storm, hitting the relaxation button on your body. That's why breathwork is so helpful—it allows you to call on the calmness you want to bring upon yourself.

By consciously slowing down your breathing, you're telling your body, "Hey, it's all good. There's no need to sound the alarm anymore." Naturally, your heart rate will follow suit, easing into a steady rhythm, and you'll feel as chill as a cucumber and be able to continue watching your favorite show. So, whether it's a sudden noise in the night or a looming deadline at work, your breath is essential against stress.

Why don't you try it right now? Take a deep breath, let it out slowly, and watch as your body and mind find their way back to Zen mode. It's like having a personal stress-relief tool kit, ready to whip out whenever life throws a curveball your way.

Speaking of tool kits, now that you understand how breathwork works and why it's helpful, it's time to explore the various breathwork techniques you can use daily.

Techniques of Breathwork

There are many brilliant breathwork techniques that can be helpful in various situations. Breathwork is all about experimentation to see which techniques are most effective at relieving stress in certain situations. Everyone is different, after all, and you can experiment to find the breathwork technique that best speaks to you in different circumstances. Up next, you'll explore seven different techniques you can try for yourself. Keep in mind that these techniques are most effective when repeated three to four times in one session, so don't give up after one go. Let's start with the 4-7-8 breathing technique.

4-7-8 Breathing Technique

Imagine this: It's the night before a big presentation, and your mind is racing with what-ifs and doubts. Have you done enough to impress the client? What if you forget the terminology or, worse, mispronounce a word? As you try to fall asleep, you realize you have two options: You can either continue to toss and turn, or you can whip out your 4-7-8 breathing technique, which will fade the worries into the background and replace them with a sense of calm and confidence. Naturally, you choose the latter.

The 4-7-8 breathing technique is a powerhouse for calming your mind and body. Originating from ancient yogic practices and brought into the mainstream by Dr. Andrew Weil, this method has proven its worth in reducing stress and anxiety (Cleveland Clinic, 2022). This technique is a real mind-soother, and it involves counting your breath. By counting your breaths, you immediately give your racing thoughts something else to focus on, effectively quieting the mental chatter. In other words, it kicks stress and anxiety to the curb by activating your body's relaxation response. The 4-7-8 breathing technique taps into your chill mode, helping you unwind and prepare for a restful sleep. Here's how you do it:

1. Start by sitting or lying down in a comfortable position.
2. Close your eyes and inhale quietly through your nose for a count of 4 seconds.
3. Hold your breath for 7 seconds.
4. Then, exhale slowly and audibly through your mouth for 8 seconds.

Throughout this breathing exercise, position your tongue toward the roof of your mouth, with the tip touching the back of your two front teeth. Also, before you start counting, be sure to start with a thorough exhale to ensure that your lungs are empty. Let your breath out through your lips and make a whooshing sound as you empty your lungs. Once that's complete, begin the steps and the counting.

Whether it's before a stressful event, during a bout of anxiety, or simply as part of your daily self-care routine, the 4-7-8 breathing technique is your ticket to peace of mind.

Box Breathing

Take a moment to imagine the following scenario: You're on your way to the class reunion, and you're feeling stressed and overwhelmed about it. Your mind is running through all the things you've yet to accomplish, dreading celebrating everyone's success while you feel inadequate. You're already on the train, so you don't feel comfortable using the 4-7-8 breathing technique, so what can you do? Introducing box breathing.

Box breathing, also known as *sama vritti pranayama*, can be used by everyone from Navy SEALs to everyday folks feeling overwhelmed. Box breathing is a mindfulness practice in itself, an opportunity to tune in to your breath and anchor yourself in the present moment. As you silently count your breaths, you're slipping into a state of meditation, quieting the mind and finding peace. It allows you to calm the storms raging within you while being discreet about it. Box breathing is essential in your breathing tool kit because it's probably one of the simplest. While some techniques might seem overwhelming to beginners, box breathing keeps it simple without sacrificing efficiency. Here's how you can do it:

1. Imagine a square with four equal sides. That's your guide for box breathing.
2. Inhale deeply for a count of 4.
3. Then, hold that breath for 4 counts.
4. Slowly exhale for another 4 counts.
5. Hold your lungs empty for the final 4 counts to complete the first box.

Remember to repeat the cycle a few times to reap the benefits fully.

Diaphragmatic Breathing

You're about to enter the exam hall to write your final and biggest exam of the year. You feel the tension building as you look around you, witnessing all the nervous faces. As your friend greets you, you notice their textbook is open on a chapter you didn't study. Panic starts to rise, and all you can hear is your own heart beating outside of your chest. Your friend kindly takes your hand and says, "Just breathe in and out."

While "just breathe in and out" might sound oversimplified, it's the key to diaphragmatic breathing. Diaphragmatic breathing, also known as deep breathing, abdominal breathing, or belly breathing, is a simple yet powerful technique for harnessing the full potential of your breath. When you breathe normally, you don't actually use your lungs to their full capacity, but diaphragmatic breathing allows you to use your lungs at 100% capacity and lung efficiency.

With diaphragmatic breathing, you fully expand your lungs,

allowing fresh air to enter. This not only oxygenates your body but also triggers a cascade of calming effects, such as a slower heart rate and reduced blood pressure (Harvard Health Publishing, 2020). Here's how you can make use of it:

1. Start by finding a comfy spot to sit or lie down.
2. Place one hand on your chest and the other just below your rib cage.
3. As you breathe in through your nose, feel your lower belly rise gently like a balloon while keeping your chest as still as possible.
4. Then, slowly exhale through your mouth, letting your belly fall back down.
5. Repeat this cycle, focusing on the rise and fall of your belly with each breath.

When you start out, practice this exercise for 5–10 minutes about three times a day. Then, gradually increase the time you spend doing the exercise. You can also increase the effort of the exercise by placing a book on your abdomen to strengthen your lung capacity further.

Alternate Nostril Breathing

Imagine for a moment you're in a heated argument with your partner. You've been going back and forth, and the disagreement is no longer headed toward a solution. Tensions are running high, and you're feeling overwhelmed and reactive. You're upset but also scared that one of you will say something you'll regret later. Instead of continuing the argument, you decide to take a brief moment away and practice alternate nostril breathing.

Alternate nostril breathing can help you regain composure, remain calm, and approach a situation with greater clarity and understanding. Also known as *Nadī Shodhana*, this technique is like a power wash for your energy channels, leaving you feeling refreshed and balanced, allowing you to enter a relaxed state. When the body is in a relaxed state, it can initiate healing and repair processes. In other words, alternate nostril breathing leaves you feeling relaxed and improves your alertness and clarity. It enables you to look beyond the chaos and the heightened emotions to find peace and calm.

Studies have shown that regular practice of alternate nostril breathing can lead to decreased stress levels (Naik et al., 2018). It has also shown that alternate nostril breathing can reduce blood pressure while boosting alertness (Telles et al., 2017). Here are the steps to practice alternate nostril breathing:

1. Raise your right hand to your nose, positioning your index finger above your left nostril and your thumb above your right nostril.
2. Close your right nostril with your thumb and inhale deeply through your left nostril.
3. Close both nostrils by pressing your index finger against your left nostril. Hold your breath for a brief moment.
4. Release your thumb to open your right nostril and exhale slowly.
5. Pause briefly at the end of your exhale.
6. Keeping your left nostril closed, inhale through your right nostril.
7. Close your right nostril with your thumb. Hold your breath briefly with both nostrils closed.
8. Release your index finger to open your left nostril and exhale slowly.

Repeat these steps for a total of 5 minutes at a time, focusing on your breath and maintaining a steady rhythm.

Pursed Lip Breathing

You're on an airplane on your way to your dream holiday destination after several months of long work hours and crazy deadlines. You can't wait to relax by the pool and enjoy time away from the office, but you can't stop wondering whether the team will be able to function properly without you. Your partner is fast asleep, and you're tempted to grab your laptop to send a few emails, even though you promised them you would relax the moment you get on the plane. You feel your breathing grow shallow, wondering if this trip was a big mistake. To make things worse, the captain announces that you should expect some slight turbulence shortly. Panicking slightly, you decide to use the pursed lip breathing technique.

The pursed lip breathing technique is one of the most straightforward methods of managing your breath and is praised for its simplicity. You might recognize it as one of the techniques athletes use to regulate their breathing pace, but it can also be very effective and beneficial for non-athletes in a sticky, stressful situation. The beauty of pursed lip breathing is that it facilitates better oxygen intake, which allows you to master your breath control (Cleveland Clinic, 2023a). It also enhances ventilation and promotes an overall state of relaxation. Here's how you can practice this technique:

1. Focus on relaxing your neck and shoulder muscles as you release the tension you might be carrying.
2. Through your nose, inhale slowly for 2 seconds, keeping your mouth closed. You don't have to take a very deep breath, so breathe as you usually would. Notice how your abdomen expands as you inhale.
3. Next, purse your lips as if you're blowing your hot coffee or trying to whistle.
4. Slowly exhale as you gently push the air through your

pursed lips for at least four seconds. As you exhale, notice your abdomen contracting.

You can repeat this breathing technique as often as you like, as it will allow you to slow down your panic and grant you the ability to enter a relaxed state of mind.

Lion's Breath

I want you to envision the following scenario for a moment: You're outside of the mall, ready for the biggest sale of the year. You're usually not one for busy environments and crowds of people, but the sales are just too good to pass up. You have your list of items you're looking for, and your shoes are laced and ready to go, but you feel this horrid dread in your stomach. Do you really want to spend your Saturday overstimulated by loud mall music and people pushing and shouting all around you? You consider going home, but you know you'll regret it later. You close your eyes and decide to use the lion's breath technique instead.

The lion's breath technique, known in Sanskrit as *Simha pranayama*, is a technique that mimics the roar of a lion. Don't worry; you don't *actually* have to roar; it simply mimics that power through your breathing. Lion's breath is a slightly less subtle breathing technique as it's characterized by its powerful nature (King of the Jungle, 2023). This technique can help you release tension and ground yourself before immersing in a potentially overwhelming situation. Not only does this technique encourage mental relaxation, but it also helps you to relax the physical tension in your face. It's also a fun and easy way to boost your confidence and self-assurance before entering a social situation (Javed & Mishra, 2022). Here's how you can do it:

1. With your back straight and your hands resting gently on your knees or thighs, become aware of your relaxed state.
2. Take a few deep breaths and focus on the present moment.
3. Inhale deeply through your nose for several counts. This will initiate the lion's breath.
4. Next, exhale and release the breath through your mouth. Extend your tongue outward and emit a "haaa" sound. Gaze softly upward to embrace the power of the lion.
5. Repeat the sequence 5–10 times, pausing between breaths to breathe normally if necessary.
6. Once you've completed your breaths, conclude the practice by breathing deeply for one minute.

At first, you might feel awkward engaging in the lion's breath method, but the more you practice it, the more at ease you'll feel. Don't shy away from your power; embrace your fierce inner lion with this technique.

Five-Finger Breathing

You're lying on your hospital bed, waiting for the nurses to roll you down the hall to surgery. As you await the surgery, you start to feel anxious as all the possible complications run through your mind. What if something goes wrong? What if the surgery makes things worse and not better? You sense the tension rise, and your chest tightens as you feel alone and terrified of what's to come. As you're struggling to breathe, you remember the five-finger breathing technique and decide to make use of it to manage your pre-operative stress and anxiety.

The five-finger breathing technique is an impactful method that offers a sense of control and calm even when you're in an unsettling environment. The beauty of this technique is that it can be practiced virtually anywhere, and it engages multiple senses at a time, not just breathing. The five-finger technique promotes the brain to release endorphins, which serve as a natural pain-relieving agent, offering immediate, natural relief. It can also alleviate stress, relax the body, enhance healing, and facilitate better sleep. Here's how you can practice it (*How Five-Finger Breathing Can Bring On Relaxed Breathing*, 2023):

1. Start by preparing your hands by designating one hand as your stationary base and the other as your tracing hand. The choice of hand for each role is up to you, but I suggest using your dominant hand as the tracing hand. Hold your base hand in front of you, face up, with your fingers comfortably spread apart.
2. Place the index finger of your tracing hand at the base of your thumb on the stationary hand where the wrist meets the arm. Move your index finger upward along the length of your thumb as you inhale and trace it back down the other side of the finger while you breathe out. Close your eyes for added focus. As you reach the tip of your thumb, exhale and drag the index finger in the opposite direction.
3. Proceed to trace each finger in a similar manner. Keep a steady breathing rhythm as you trace the fingers up and down.
4. Once you reach the base of your last finger, the pinky, reverse the direction and trace each finger back toward your thumb. Remain mindful of your breathing as you focus on the sensation of your finger moving across your skin. With each exhale, release a little more tension as you allow yourself to relax.
5. Repeat for as long as you need to. When you feel calm,

gently open your eyes and carry that relaxed feeling with you.

If you're new to five-finger breathing, consider using guided audio or video to assist you initially. Once you're comfortable with the technique, you can practice it independently whenever you need to unwind.

Using Breathwork in Your Everyday Life

All of these breathing techniques are wonderful, but there is a time and place for each. Not all techniques are suitable for every situation. For example, it might not be a great idea to let out an audible "haaa" while waiting to enter an interview or to close your eyes and trace your fingers while you're stuck in traffic. You need to consider a couple of things when incorporating these techniques into your daily life.

First, consider your needs. Are you looking to calm down or increase focus? You should also consider your immediate surroundings. Are you alone or in the middle of an important meeting? Finally, consider how much time you have to practice breathing. Do you need a quick calm-me-down, or are you worried about something hours from now? By considering all these points, you'll have a good idea of which technique to use.

The 4-7-8 technique is a fun pocket-size stress reliever that doesn't require a lot of time or resources, allowing you to use it more often. On the other hand, the five-finger breathing technique is a bit more hands-on (literally), but it's ideal for when you have a quiet moment to yourself and are not in a rush.

At the end of the day, it's all about what works best for you in every situation. Take your time to practice each technique and note how it makes you feel, how subtle it is, and how long it takes you. That way, you'll know which technique to rely on and when. Once you've dipped your toes into the world of breathwork techniques, don't be afraid to test the waters with a few different ones. It's all about finding what clicks best with you. And hey, if your go-to method isn't hitting the spot or you're just craving a bit of variety, there's a whole buffet of options waiting for you to explore.

As you continue learning how to relax and use these different techniques, here are a few tips that might make it a little easier:

- **Find your Zen zone:** When starting out with relaxation techniques, make sure you find a space that is your Zen zone. Whether it's a cozy corner of your living room or a patch of grass in the park, pick a spot where you can truly unwind without any distractions. Eventually, you'll be able to practice these wherever you are, but this tip will help you at the beginning of your breathwork journey.
- **Keep it chill:** Relaxation isn't a race, so don't stress yourself out trying to force it. Take things slow and let the relaxation flow naturally.
- **Stay engaged:** While relaxation is about letting go, it's also about staying present. Find a focal point, whether it's a soothing mantra or the feeling of your breath, to keep you anchored in the moment.
- **Make it a habit:** Consistency is key when it comes to relaxation. Try to carve out time for your practice each day, ideally at the same time, to build up that sense of routine.
- **Focus on quality over quantity:** You don't need to dedicate hours on end to reap the benefits of relaxation. Even 10-20 minutes a day can work wonders for your well-being.

Incorporating breathwork techniques into your daily routine can be a game-changer for managing stress. By tapping into the power of breathwork, you can activate your body's natural relaxation response, reduce stress hormones, and promote a sense of calm. Whether it's a quick fix for a stressful moment or a daily practice for overall well-being, breathwork offers a simple yet profound tool for dealing with life's challenges with greater ease.

The next chapter will explore the second S-I-M-P-L-E framework strategy, diving into intrapersonal communication and how you talk to yourself. Get ready to turn your worst critic into your best friend as you learn to speak to yourself with kindness and compassion.

5

INTRAPERSONAL COMMUNICATION— SELF-TALK AND SELF-COMPASSION

EVERYONE TALKS to themselves internally on a daily basis, but did you know *how* you talk to yourselves can significantly impact your well-being? Take a moment to consider your internal dialogue. Are you kind and supportive? Or, do you tend to become the villain in your own story, tearing yourself down at every opportunity? The words you speak to yourself can shape your thoughts, feelings, and actions, and this chapter will explore how.

Once you understand that the way you speak to yourself can influence your well-being, you can begin to take action and speak positivity into your life. But before jumping into the how, you first need to acknowledge the importance of accepting your emotions. When you can accept your emotions, you are more likely to speak to yourself in a kind and caring manner. Let's take a look at that right now.

Accepting Your Emotions

Emotions can often feel like a heavy boulder that you have to carry up a hill, but they can also be a very powerful source of growth and survival. Your body communicates with you through your emotions, and while it can sometimes feel overwhelming, there's always something you can learn from it. That's why it's crucial to acknowledge that emotions matter and accept them, as they can contribute to your psychological well-being. At the end of the day, emotions are inevitable, and you'll always experience them.

Failing to accept your emotions can lead to long-term pain and cause negativity in your life. When you accept your feelings, you are actually less likely to react negatively to stress. By accepting your feelings, chances are you'll think first and act later once you've processed all the information (Elmer, 2022). The problem arises when you ignore your emotions or judge yourself because of the emotions you're feeling. In many cultures, acknowledging feelings is a weakness, which can lead to various stigmas surrounding emotions. However, at the core of human behavior, emotions are natural, and it is beneficial to express them.

When you judge your emotions, it can easily lead to negative self-talk. You might get mad at yourself for feeling a certain way or put pressure on yourself to accept something that you're not okay with. This can lead to denial, which always backfires. Avoidance might bring short-term relief, but it will only increase stress later on. The problem is that avoidance can also seep into other areas of your life where you'll soon be avoiding anything that might stir up emotions. Trying to avoid negative emotions is like trying to stop a flood with your bare hands. You'll end up permanently on edge, constantly on the lookout for any signs of negative emotions, only to get overwhelmed when the flood hits. In the end, it will cause way more stress than the original emotions you tried to avoid.

When you accept stressful emotions, something incredible happens: you gain the opportunity to combine mindfulness with exploration and curiosity. When you are curious about your emotions, you will understand why you are feeling certain things. This can lead to self-compassion, acceptance, and the ability to deal

INTRAPERSONAL COMMUNICATION—SELF-TALK AND SELF-... 51

with stress. Imagine for a moment you're feeling panicked as you walk into the workplace and are unsure why. Instead of avoiding it, you acknowledge and accept that you're feeling that way, which leads you to wonder why. You identify that you're feeling panicked because yesterday, when you walked in, a coworker said something rude to you, and now your subconscious is scared that it might happen again. By accepting that you're panicked, you can show yourself compassion and not judgment for feeling that way. In other words, accepting your emotions is a crucial step for feeling comfortable with your emotions, aiding in stress relief. Let's explore strategies to make this happen.

Strategies to Accept Your Emotions

When you're in the heat of the moment, and your emotions are all over the place, it can feel like you're riding a roller coaster with no seatbelt. But it doesn't have to feel that way. With the right strategies and techniques, you can accept and embrace your emotions without giving them all the control. By facing your emotions, you have a better chance at controlling them in a healthy manner rather than letting them control you. Let's take a look at a few different techniques, starting with grounding techniques.

Grounding Techniques

Grounding techniques are mental exercises that help bring you back to the present moment and reduce anxiety by focusing on your senses and surroundings. You can use many different grounding techniques, including the **5, 4, 3, 2, 1 technique**. Let's try it right now:

1. Look around the room and name five things you can see, five things you can hear, and five things you can feel.

2. Then, repeat the exercise, searching for four things, then three, and so on, until you're looking for one thing in each category.

This technique will allow you to let go of the immediate emotions and allow your subconscious to process what happened. It will also force you to pause before acting on the emotion.

Next, let's try the **naming categories technique:**

1. Pick a category, for example colors or shapes, then name all the things around you that fit into that category.

Again, this strategy will allow you to pause and breathe before you do something that you'll regret later.

Another helpful method is the **cold water technique:**

1. Take a few slow sips of cold water and focus on the sensation in your mouth and throat.

This gives your mind something to think about other than ruminating over the negative emotions you're experiencing.

Emotion Surfing

Emotion surfing is a strategy that can help you ride the waves of your emotions instead of getting knocked over by them. When you're feeling a strong emotion, instead of trying to push it away or control it, you simply observe it. Notice how it feels in your body, what thoughts are swirling around in your head, and any urges you might have to react. Remember, emotions come and go like waves in the ocean. They might feel intense at first, but they always pass eventually. By surfing through your emotions, you learn to tolerate the distress and let it ebb away naturally (McKay & West, 2016).

During an emotion-surfing session, you can ask questions like, "What do I notice happening in my body right now?" or "What thoughts are popping into my head?" Once you've asked these questions, allow your feelings to simmer without the need to "get over" them. It's all about exploring your emotional experience with curiosity and without judgment. By doing so, you'll begin to notice that your emotions are valid, but they don't have to be overwhelming. The more you practice emotion surfing, the better you'll get at accepting and tolerating your feelings.

Soften, Soothe, and Allow Technique

Next is the soften, soothe, and allow technique. This technique can be incredibly beneficial and is fairly simple to try. Here's how to get started:

1. Start by finding a comfy spot and taking a couple of deep breaths.
2. Think about what's bothering you and focus on how it makes you feel.
3. Identify the strongest emotions you are feeling and notice how your body responds. Do you feel tightness in your chest or perhaps a knot in your stomach?
4. For the softening phase, imagine your emotions like a swimming pool, and you choose to let go of the ledge.
5. Now, effortlessly float in your emotions. Place your hand on the spot where you feel the emotion and soothe yourself by offering yourself kind words of comfort.
6. Remind yourself that it's okay to feel this way and that no emotions are wrong. Allow your emotions to flow through you without judgment.
7. Keep checking in with your body to notice any change in

the sensations. Notice how the water in the swimming pool gently washes your stress away.
8. When you're ready for the allow phase, place your hand over your heart and send yourself some love and compassion. Remember, we're all just doing our best, and it's okay to be imperfect.

When dealing with emotions, these techniques form part of your tool kit. What works for one person might not work for another, so it's all about finding what clicks for you. Keep experimenting and see which one feels like the best fit for you.

Benefits of Positive Self-Talk

These techniques to manage and accept your emotions enable you to embrace positive self-talk. Self-talk is exactly what it sounds like—it's the way you communicate with yourself. Imagine speaking to your friends the way you speak to yourself internally. Would you be a good friend, or would they consider you mean and uncaring? If it's the latter, it says a lot about the current state of your self-talk. Take a moment to imagine gearing up for a big presentation. All the signs of classic stress are there: sweaty palms, racing heart, etc. Your self-talk can take one of two directions:

- It can either yell and scream, convincing you that you're about to fail because you're not good enough and don't deserve success, or
- It can help calm you down, reminding you that you're only human and that jitters are normal; you've prepared for this and are ready.

Which one do you think will have the better outcome? But self-talk isn't about slapping a band-aid on your stress; it's about digging deeper and uncovering those buried positive emotions. Maybe you've been so caught up in the nerves that you forgot how stoked you are about your topic or how proud you are of the hard work you've put in. Self-talk enables you to calm down, picture a positive outcome, and acknowledge feelings without judgment, boosting your confidence along the way.

Self-Talk Techniques

Now that you understand the importance of self-talk and how it relates to your emotion regulation and stress, it's time to explore some techniques to help you embrace positive self-talk more.

Perceived Stress Scale

The Perceived Stress Scale (PSS) was developed by Dr. Sheldon Cohen and his colleagues at Carnegie Mellon University. This scale measures how overwhelmed you feel by the stress in your life (Greenberg, 2017). High perceived stress is like a neon sign pointing toward a host of health issues—from heart disease to depression. But here's the flip side: Finding ways to dial down that stress-o-meter can be a game-changer for both your mind and body.

But why does it matter how you perceive stress? Think of it like this: If you're convinced you're facing an apocalypse every time a stressful situation shows up, your body's stress response system stays stuck in overdrive, and your self-talk will contribute to the chaos. Even after the stressors have passed and you've successfully finished the presentation, your parasympathetic nervous system will still work overtime to get your mind to calm down. This can cause self-talk such as, "Why were you so stressed in the first place? You're so weak!" By speaking to yourself in such a way, you'll only jump-start the amygdala back up, convinced that it's still facing a stressor. On the other hand, with positive self-talk, you can motivate yourself and be reminded that stress is normal and that it doesn't make you weak.

So, when you feel stressed, take a deep breath and hit yourself with self-talk. Maybe it sounds like this: "Hey, stress, thanks for the heads-up! Now, let's assess the situation. Do I need to tackle this head-on, or can I let it slide?" It's like giving yourself a pep talk, but instead of hyping yourself up for a big game, you're calming yourself down in the face of stress. And guess what? You're in control here. You get to decide how you react to stress. If you're not sure how stressed you feel or why you are overwhelmed, the perceived stress scale is a great place to start.

Worst Case Scenario

Next, it's time to get into the specific phrases and techniques of self-talk that will help you manage your stress in the short-term. When stress starts creeping in, your brain is quick to jump straight to the worst-case scenarios. You know the drill—you've got a speech to give or a tough conversation on the horizon, and suddenly, your mind is conjuring up all sorts of catastrophic outcomes. Instead of fighting the thoughts, you can allow your brain to do its thing and ask yourself, "What's the absolute worst that can happen?" Let's use the following scenario to put it into practice:

Let's say you're stressing because you're running late to your kid's swimming class. What's the worst that could happen? Maybe your kiddo misses the warm-up or gets a puzzled look from the instructor when you walk in late. Is that really so bad? Maybe the instructor won't even care because they're too busy teaching the other kids, and then all the stress was for nothing. Once you embrace the worst-case scenarios, they lose their power over you. Suddenly, being a few minutes late to swimming class doesn't seem so earth-shattering.

Everything Happens for a Reason

This self-talk gem works wonders, and it's as simple as reminding yourself that "Everything happens for a reason." Once you internalize this mantra, stress loses its grip over you. If you're stuck in traffic and running late for that swim class, remind yourself that everything happens for a reason. Maybe if you had left earlier, you would've ended up in a fender-bender or stuck in gridlock traffic. Suddenly, being a tad late to swimming class feels like a minor blip on the radar, and this one saying can even result in you being grateful that something worse didn't happen.

The Control Issue

When you look inside your mind and explore why you feel stressed and anxious, you'll find that a lot of it has to do with control. You freak out whenever you feel out of control, and your self-talk reflects that. It's like you have a little guy inside your head, running around and screaming, "You idiot! We've lost all control! Code red!" You give a lot of your emotional power to control, and the moment you lose control, your emotions flip out. But what would happen if you didn't fight to gain control and accepted that there are things you simply can't control? You'll have a much calmer outlook on life.

By acknowledging that something is out of your control, you subconsciously accept that there is only so much you can do about it. A lot of stress occurs when you try to control things you can't and fail to focus on the things you can actually control. Instead of being stressed about your manager's opinion of your presentation, which is something you have no control over, you can switch your focus to refining your speech and practice it out loud, which is something you can control. By doing so, you'll feel calmer and less stressed.

When you're stressed, take a moment and ask yourself whether it's something you can control. If it's not, remind yourself of it by practicing supportive self-talk. For example, "I can't control whether I get the promotion next year, but I can control my behavior leading up to it." A tool that can be very helpful with this task is the worry box. The worry box is a physical box where you keep everything you're worried about but can't necessarily control. It's a safe space for your worries to hang out without disrupting the rest of your mind. Writing your worries out on a piece of paper and placing them in the worry box allows you to focus on the worries you can control, which is very empowering.

You can also schedule "worry times" in your day in which you allow yourself a couple of minutes to consider these situations. That way, you acknowledge what you're feeling but accept that it's out of your control. Ultimately, it all boils down to one thing: assessing the situation and deciding whether it's within your control or not. Once you've got that clarity, you'll know which path to take—whether it's embracing the uncertainty or taking charge and making things happen.

Will This Impact Me Tomorrow?

Sometimes, people tend to worry about things that are only temporary. They get embarrassed, scared, or panicked by something that won't influence our present or future in the slightest. Stressful situations can feel overwhelming, but you can practice self-talk by reminding yourself that it's only temporary. You can even ask yourself the question: "Will this matter tomorrow or next week?" If the answer is no, it will immediately put things into perspective and help you to calm the stressful voice in your head.

When you're stressed and realize it won't matter tomorrow or next week (or perhaps even in an hour), take a deep breath and find solace, knowing it will be over soon. That presentation you're fretting over? A week from now, it'll be a distant memory. Worried about that upcoming exam? Soon, it'll be conquered and behind you. By reminding yourself of this, you can find comfort in knowing that time will keep marching forward, carrying you along with it.

Self-Compassion

Self-talk and self-compassion are closely related, and you can't have one without the other. Self-compassion is treating yourself with kindness and understanding, even when you feel like you've messed up or are feeling super stressed about something. When you talk to yourself from a place of self-compassion, you can show yourself kindness, which will contribute to embracing a supportive self-talk voice instead of an inner critic.

When stress hits, that inner critic can be relentless, pushing you to work harder, do more, and never cut yourself some slack. But with self-compassion, you'll be able to break free from the cycle and remember that there are many things you are good at and that you're worthy of being treated with kindness. So, how can you embrace self-compassion on a daily basis? Let's have a look:

- Start by noticing how you talk to yourself, especially when you make a mistake or feel down. Would you speak to a friend that way? Replace harsh words with self-compassionate support.
- Engage in activities that bring you comfort and relaxation. This could be taking a warm bath, reading a favorite book, spending time in nature, or listening to calming music.
- When you're feeling overwhelmed or stressed, take a mindful pause. Focus on your breathing, acknowledge your emotions without judgment, and remind yourself that this challenging feeling is temporary.
- Take a moment each day to appreciate the good things in

your life, big or small. This could be anything from being grateful for your health to savoring a delicious meal.
- Holding onto anger and resentment, especially toward yourself, hinders self-compassion. Acknowledge your mistakes, learn from them, and let go. Remember, everyone makes mistakes, and forgiveness allows you to move forward with kindness toward yourself.

Speaking to yourself with compassion isn't something you should see as a luxury but as a necessity. The way you talk to yourself will not only affect how you manage stress but also boost your confidence and help you in other areas of your life.

Acquiring this new skill of talking to yourself with kindness will greatly benefit the next technique of the S-I-M-P-L-E framework: mindfulness.

6

MINDFULNESS

A FEW YEARS AGO, I sat across from my husband at the dinner table and started sobbing uncontrollably. Overwhelmed by my daily tasks and constantly feeling busy, yet not feeling satisfied with life, I had lost all hope. "I'm constantly juggling a million things, but I never feel truly present," I cried. Even as I sat there crying, I was thinking about how I didn't have time to cry because I still had to put away all the kids' toys scattered throughout the house and remember to remove the clothes from the dryer. This little breakdown happened before I encountered the wonderful world of mindfulness and yoga. I felt stuck in a loop of stress and chaos, seeing no way through it.

Have you ever felt like that before? Like you're constantly busy and don't have time for hobbies or relaxation? And when you finally get to your hobbies, you're already thinking of all the other endless tasks you have to do. It can be overwhelming and debilitating. But let me share some good news with you: There's a way out, and it's called mindfulness. Chances are, you've heard something about mindfulness recently. It's become quite the buzzword on social media due to its myriad benefits. But there's more to it than just being a trend, and that's exactly what this chapter will explore.

It will start with the basics as it explores what mindfulness is and its benefits. Next, it will examine what you want to achieve with mindfulness, along with techniques to do so. Finally, it will demonstrate mindfulness meditation and how you can implement mindfulness into your day-to-day life. Get ready to jump into the wonderful world of mindfulness as the third S-I-M-P-L-E framework strategy available to you to manage stress more effectively. Let's start by asking the question, "What is mindfulness?"

What Is Mindfulness?

Over the last few years, mindfulness-based interventions have gained popularity among therapists, educators, coaches, and even politicians. But it's definitely not a new movement, as it's been around for many, many years. The origin of mindfulness can be traced back to ancient Eastern traditions and religions, and Buddhism heavily influences it. Luckily for the rest of the world, mindfulness made its way across the globe, mainly through the work of Professor Jon Kabat-Zinn.

Kabat-Zinn was a renowned scientist and practitioner who introduced mindfulness as a therapeutic intervention in the late 1970s. He drew inspiration from the Buddhists and developed Mindfulness-Based Stress Reduction (MBSR). He focused on helping alleviate suffering, including chronic pain and stress-related conditions (Mindful, 2021). Kabat-Zinn defined mindfulness as paying attention purposefully, without judgment, and accepting the present moment (Greenberg, 2016).

Through his studies, Kabat-Zinn and his team demonstrated the efficacy of mindfulness in enhancing psychological well-being and physical health. They found that MBSR participants experienced significant reductions in symptoms associated with anxiety, depression, chronic pain, and insomnia. These results added to the popularity of mindfulness, and it quickly became the go-to method for many people. Since then, mindfulness has grown and expanded to all corners of the world, and many practitioners use it in their treatment plans.

It's important to recognize that mindfulness isn't something that happens overnight. It takes time to cultivate mindfulness, and while mindfulness practices might offer immediate benefits in stress management, the real power comes when you embrace mindfulness as a long-term lifestyle. With consistency, mindfulness can be an essential tool to overcome stress and help you develop healthy coping mechanisms. Mindfulness isn't something you do once, and then it's complete; it's something you work on daily. That's why it's essential to integrate mindfulness into your daily life through simple practices. It doesn't have to be complex as long as you gradually build resilience and emotional intelligence, which are essential skills to develop when learning to manage stress better.

Benefits of Mindfulness

If you take a moment to scroll through TikTok or Instagram reels, chances are you'll probably come across hashtag mindfulness in the first few minutes. It's become quite a trend, especially since so many people feel the need for it. But mindfulness isn't a passing trend; it's a scientifically proven approach to enhancing well-being and reducing stress. For more than two decades, researchers have been using advanced technology to measure the benefits of mindfulness.

There is growing evidence that mindfulness training can physically influence the amygdala, the alarm system in the brain discussed in Chapters 1 and 2. As you know, the amygdala is a key brain region for processing emotions, especially stress and fear. When you're stressed, the amygdala lights up with activity, which can cause negative stimuli. However, research has shown that mindfulness practices can decrease the negative activity of the amygdala, dampening the stress response and allowing you to feel calmer.

Mindfulness can also strengthen the prefrontal cortex, which you know plays a part in reigning in the panicky amygdala. By strengthening the prefrontal cortex, mindfulness allows you to think rationally, make informed decisions, and reduce reactivity triggered by stress and fear. In other words, instead of freaking out before your mother-in-law comes over, mindfulness will help you to identify ways to ensure the visit goes well (Hsu, 2023). The benefits of mindfulness show up in various other ways, such as:

- stress reduction
- improved mental health
- enhanced focus and concentration
- better emotional regulation
- improved physical health
- increased self-awareness
- reduced symptoms of depression and anxiety
- decreased feelings of overwhelm
- limited rumination and mind-wandering
- weight management
- lowered blood pressure and cortisol levels

In other words, yes, mindfulness is definitely worth a try, considering it can do so many wonderful things for your health, physically and mentally. The best part is that it's all based on science, not just a good feeling.

What State Are You Trying to Achieve?

Chances are, if you're reading this book, you're feeling stressed. When you're in a state of stress, your amygdala reacts to all the perceived threats in real time, which triggers the fight, flight, or freeze response. I know this isn't new information, but it's crucial to understand that it's the fight, flight, or freeze response that can make you feel overwhelmed, panicked, and paralyzed by your stress levels. To fight stressed states, people often rely on unhealthy coping mechanisms that offer temporary relief but never long-term. That's where mindfulness offers a new way out of the cycle that provides not just immediate relief but also a long-term solution.

Mindfulness offers a new perspective, a state of calm and peace. It allows your amygdala's reactivity to take a break as it restores your mind and body balance. The goal isn't to erase all your stressful thoughts or remove the amygdala's fight, flight, or freeze responses entirely. Instead, it allows you to change your relationship with your stress. This can be done by achieving a mindful state. Let's take a moment to explore the characteristics of the mindful state. Just like people, you can learn a lot about a strategy by exploring its characteristics and its purpose in your life.

In *The Stress-Proof Brain* by Melanie Greenberg (2016), there are seven characteristics of a mindful state of mind. Let's take a closer look and inspect whether any of these characteristics resonate with you, and what you are ultimately trying to achieve through practicing mindfulness.

The Observer

The first characteristic of a mindful state of mind is that you become an observer of your own feelings. You no longer feel consumed by them, and you also won't feel the urge to push them away. Instead, it provides you with mental space and freedom to observe your stress from an outsider's point of view, giving you more control over your reactions to your stressful state.

The "Being" Over "Doing" Solution

The mindful state emphasizes "being" over "doing." When you're stressed, your brain might jump to problem-solving mode and encourage you to take action immediately. However, sometimes, it's important to just be in the moment and experience the present without trying to find a solution. It's like telling your friend a story, and they immediately offer solutions when all you wanted was to vent a little bit. By focusing on "being" over "doing," you allow your brain to reset your mental reserves (Schenck, 2011).

The Slow Down Captain

Have you ever felt so anxious that it seemed like the world was running at double speed? Perhaps you've been so stressed that it feels like you are racing to solve a problem you don't yet understand. Well, that's all thanks to your friend, the one and only amygdala. When you are stressed, the brain runs in overdrive, and it tries to solve the stressors with immediate action. While this is life-saving when you're stuck in a burning building, not all stressors can be solved in such a way. Luckily, mindfulness deliberately slows down the thought process. It gives your prefrontal cortex enough time to assess and respond accordingly by removing the urgency.

The Equanimity Teacher

The mindful state is all about gaining peace, balance, and equanimity. This means that you let go of the need for things to be done in a specific way, removing the fear of failure and the feeling of panic that things won't be done correctly. Instead, mindfulness allows you to remain in control and find the balance between doing your best and accepting that there is no such thing as perfection. This is a world where everything constantly changes, and by accepting that, you'll let go of the fear of lack of control.

The Non-Judgmental Friend

The mindful state heavily highlights the importance of being non-judgmental toward yourself and your stressors. Instead of labeling things in your life as good or bad, the mindful state encourages seeing things as truths (Schenck, 2011). Regardless of whether it might have a positive or negative effect on you, all things are considered neutral, and you can decide what you would like to do with it. This transforms your stress by removing the sense of terror and panic.

The Present Moment Ambassador

The mindful state of mind encourages focusing on the present moment instead of living in a constant state of panic about what might happen. It allows you to be grounded in the here and the now, breaking free from rumination. By focusing on your immediate sensory experience, such as what you see, hear, or smell, you teach your mind not to think too far ahead or to get stuck in the past, which fosters a calm atmosphere to navigate stressors more effectively.

The Fear Replacement

Another characteristic of mindfulness is replacing fear with curiosity. Rather than being consumed by fear or emotional reactivity, mindfulness invites an open, spacious curiosity about thoughts and feelings. This curiosity allows you to observe your experiences without judgment, fostering a sense of peace and acceptance. You can do this by asking yourself questions about your fear instead of avoiding it (Schenck, 2011).

In essence, mindfulness offers a transformative way of relating to stress. Do you remember the earlier chapters that discussed the difference between focused mode and default mode? Mindfulness allows you to remain in focused mode. By being in focused mode, you can train your mind to focus on the present instead of jumping down the rabbit hole of what could've been or might still come. The intention is to help you remain in the present moment without being weighed down by fear of the future or regrets of the past.

Amit Sood outlines this concept of remaining in the focused mode in his book *The Mayo Clinic Guide to Stress-Free Living* (2013). He states that to remain in the present moment and find more meaningful moments in everyday life, you need to implement joyful attention and kind attention. Let's take a closer look at these techniques to achieve a mindful state.

Techniques to Achieve Mindfulness

Various mindfulness techniques can help you achieve a mindful state in your daily life. First, let's explore the two techniques suggested by Amit Sood: joyful attention and kind attention. After these two techniques, let's also look at three other techniques: refining interpretations, the wheel of awareness, and the STOP technique.

Joyful Attention

I want you to imagine this scenario for a quick second: You are standing in line at your favorite coffee shop behind two friends. It's clear that they both had a pretty rough morning and are feeling overwhelmed with all the negativity of the day. They place their order, and you watch as the barista puts extra effort into creating beautiful foam art on their lattes. You catch a glimpse of the art and are immediately amazed by the detail of the foamy flowers on top of the coffees. You watch closely as the first friend grabs her cup, stirs in some sugar, and slaps a lid on without even noticing the art. However, the second friend notices the flower. She takes out her phone and captures a photo before thanking the barista, exclaiming how this has made her day. She leaves the coffee shop in high spirits, grateful for the small pocket of joy.

I think most people tend to be like the first friend in the story, especially in their daily lives. Everyone is so busy that they totally miss the small moments of joy that present themselves. Joyful attention is all about focusing on the little things that make life beautiful and meaningful, like noticing your favorite vintage car while driving in traffic or admiring the colorful flowers near your parking spot. It's recommended that you practice joyful attention 4–8 times a day to initially train your mind to spot the joyful moments (Sood, 2013). Eventually, your mind will respond naturally as joyful attention becomes part of your subconscious mind. Here are a few ways that you can be intentional about cultivating joyful attention:

- Kick off your mornings with gratitude by focusing on the small joys, like the taste of your coffee or the warmth of your shower.
- Take a moment to connect with nature daily, soaking in its beauty and serenity.
- When you see your loved ones, greet them excitedly as if you are reuniting after ages.
- Remember to smile in the mirror—it's like giving your brain a little high-five! The "Laughter" chapter will dive deeper into that.

Kind Attention

Did you know that your brain only takes a tenth of a second to craft a judgment about someone? It's true. When you meet someone for the first time or see a stranger walking toward you, it only takes a tenth of a second for your brain to decide whether it's a foe or a friend (Sood, 2013). The problem isn't that you make these judgments. Your brain is wired to judge and to do so quickly to ensure your safety. But the problem arises when you're so set on the judgment that it creates stress. Truth be told, that split-second judgment can't possibly be accurate all the time, but people often hold on to the judgment, which slowly drains them. So, what's the antidote to judgment? Kindness.

Suppose you're out and about, and you spot someone. Before any judgment or thought pops into your head, pause and embrace the CALF method (Sood, 2013):

- **Compassion:** Understand that everyone's fighting a battle.
- **Acceptance:** Hold off on those negative judgments and give people space just to exist.
- **Love:** Imagine them surrounded by love; maybe even include yourself in that circle.
- **Forgiveness:** Let go of any minor annoyances they might have caused.

Kind attention is like a sweet exchange of positive energy. Your eyes gather information and beam out good vibes simultaneously. If eye contact feels a bit much, don't sweat it. You can just send that optimistic thought their way. This practice is all about silent sweetness. There is no need for a loud "Bless you!" Think of it like a tiny prayer, a quick wish for healing, comfort, success, or just some warm fuzzies. And remember, it's a journey—start small with those you love or feel compassion for and gradually spread that kindness far and wide.

Refining Interpretations

Your experiences and how you see the world start with what grabs your attention and how you interpret that information. It's like crafting your own story from the bits and pieces you notice around you. Now, these interpretations are heavily influenced by your present-moment preferences, which, in turn, are shaped by your past experiences, biases, and principles.

That's where prejudice comes in. Prejudices are quick judgments that your mind makes without taking the time to really process all the facts. Luckily, prejudices aren't the only ones running the show, as you also have principles. Principles come from deep introspection, guiding you with timeless wisdom. This is where gratitude, compassion, acceptance, higher meaning, and forgiveness influence the way you see the world around you instead of your immediate prejudice.

On the one hand, untrained interpretations formed primarily on the basis of prejudice can pull you into a self-serving whirlwind of thoughts—stressful, self-focused, and just plain exhausting. On the other hand, trained interpretations, guided by your trusty principles, can lead you to a calm, healing haven. It's like having a wise mentor whisper sweet nuggets of wisdom in your ear, guiding you through life's roller coaster ride.

So, how do you put these principles into action? Let me introduce you to the art of daily themes. You can assign each day of the week its own special focus, like a mini adventure. These themes can include gratitude, compassion, acceptance, higher meaning, forgiveness, or any other theme you want to focus on.

For example, one day can be themed on gratitude, the other on compassion, and so on. Now, with practice, these principles become second nature, like adding lemon and mint to your water. They change the flavor of our days, infusing them with a sense of peace, joy, and resilience. So, grab your daily theme calendar and start crafting a life filled with gratitude, compassion, acceptance, higher meaning, and forgiveness.

Wheel of Awareness

Dr. Dan Diegel introduced the Wheel of Awareness as a powerful mindfulness tool that can improve your overall well-being (Browne, 2021). Imagine for a moment you have a wheel around you, and at the center of the wheel, you have a hub where everything happens. This hub is the epicenter of your being, surrounded by other rims. The rims are where you find everything that you're aware of, including your senses, body, thoughts, and others around you.

By envisioning life as this wheel, you'll be able to plop yourself right in the cozy hub and become aware of the world around you at a deeper level than before. Start by taking a deep breath and let yourself sink into stillness. Next, send out spokes of intention from the hub to each rim. Each spoke takes you on a journey through a different segment of your total being, kind of like exploring different rooms in your own house.

Let's start with your senses—grounding yourself in the present moment by tuning into what you see, touch, hear, taste, and smell. It's like playing a game of "I Spy" with the universe, soaking in all the little details that make life so deliciously rich.

Next up is the body scan—a little check-in with your body from head to toe. Release any tension you find along the way, and listen closely to what your body is trying to tell you.

Then, there is the sea of mental activities—thoughts, emotions, memories, dreams, you name it. Instead of trying to control or suppress them, just let them flow like a river. Be the calm observer in the midst of the storm, asking yourself curious questions and noticing any patterns that emerge.

And finally, zoom out to focus on your connection to the world around you—your friends, family, community, and beyond. Set an intention to cultivate compassion, both for others and for yourself. After all, we're all in this crazy adventure called life together, right?

As you journey through each segment, let yourself be guided by curiosity and kindness, and when you're ready to wrap things up, just retreat back to that cozy hub of awareness, soaking in the peace and stillness of the present moment. Remember, this practice isn't just a one-time thing—it's a tool you can use anytime, anywhere, to tap into that deep well of inner peace and mindfulness. So, whenever life starts to feel a little too hectic, just hop on the Wheel of Awareness and let it guide you back to the center.

The STOP Technique

The last mindfulness technique I want to introduce is the STOP technique. This technique aims to create time in your day where you stop, calm your worrying mind, and reconnect to the present moment. When you use the STOP technique, you actively pause what you're doing to create a moment of clarity and perspective to regulate your response to the pressure and stress you're experiencing (Ferguson, 2009). The beauty of this technique is that it can be done at any time, and it can be especially helpful when you're stressed, upset, or angry. Here are the four steps of STOP:

- **S—Stop what you're doing:** This is the first and most crucial step. When you feel overwhelmed or stressed, literally stop what you're doing. Pause that conversation, put down your work, or step away from whatever has your attention.
- **T—Take a breath:** Take a few deep, conscious breaths. Feel your stomach expand as you inhale and slowly release the tension as you exhale. Chapter 4 covered breathing, so feel free to check that out again as a reminder.

- **O—Observe:** Notice what's happening inside you without judgment. Are you feeling tense? Is your heart racing? Are there any worries swirling in your mind? Observe your thoughts, emotions, and any physical sensations in your body.
- **P—Proceed:** With a newfound sense of calm and awareness, choose how to move forward. Do you need to address the situation differently? Do you need a few more moments to collect yourself? The key is to act with intention rather than impulsively reacting.

Now that you've explored these five techniques to achieve mindfulness, it's time to explore another aspect of mindfulness that can be helpful in many situations: mindfulness meditation.

Mindfulness Meditation

Take a moment to imagine yourself in a hammock on the porch of a luxury resort overlooking the ocean. You have nothing on your agenda for the day other than to relax, read that book you've been dying to get into, and drink as many complimentary cocktails as your heart desires. It's a total moment of relaxation. You don't have to worry about traffic, packing lunches, sorting out dinner, doing washing, or even making your own bed. Sounds like heaven, right? What if I told you that you can experience such relaxation right where you are? "How?" you might wonder. Let's get into it.

Mindfulness meditation as a technique is often overlooked when discussing other effective treatments to manage stress, but many studies have proof of its success. I found one study in particular very interesting. In 2002, the William E. Donaldson Correctional Facility (a maximum-security state prison west of Birmingham) decided to offer inmates the opportunity to experience peace and calm without the use of drugs. They organized a ten-day meditation retreat, where prisoners could choose whether to partake. After the retreat, the inmates who attended continued their practices, and the results were life-changing. The study found a decrease in recidivism and an increase in better behavior and coping skills. In fact, the inmates showed a 20% reduction in disciplinary action (Sood, 2013).

Meditation can be defined in many ways, but words fail to truly capture its essence. Like a delicious plate of food, you can try to explain it, but only by experiencing it for yourself can you truly understand the nature. Meditation promotes relaxation and a heightened sense of well-being (Sood, 2013). The goal is not to empty your mind but to focus on something specific without stress or fear distracting you. During meditation, you focus your attention on something specific, like your breath or a mantra. This helps to anchor your mind in the present moment.

Over time, this practice strengthens your ability to stay present and aware in everyday life. You become more skilled at noticing your thoughts, feelings, and sensations without getting caught up in them. It's like developing a superpower of inner calm and clarity. You can make use of anchors to help you find deep relaxation. Anchors, such as breath or sensations within your body, help steady the mind, and as you use meditation more often, you won't need anchors to help you achieve present-moment awareness.

Benefits of Meditation

Now that you have a better understanding of mindfulness meditation, you can explore the benefits it can have:

- **Reduces stress:** Mindfulness meditation can act as a stress buffer, equipping you with tools to stay calm and collected during challenging situations. By focusing on the present moment and letting go of worries about the future or regrets about the past, you can cultivate a sense of inner peace and emotional resilience (Ginexi et al., 2022).

- **Preserves the aging brain:** Meditation is the answer if you want to keep your brain young. Research suggests meditation may be like a brain gym, helping to slow cognitive decline and improve memory by strengthening the connections between brain cells. This can lead to sharper thinking, better focus, and enhanced learning abilities even as you age (Walton, 2015).
- **Manages pain:** If you want to manage your pain naturally, mindfulness can be a powerful tool. It can help you shift your focus away from the physical discomfort and towards a more accepting state of mind. By observing your pain without judgment, you can learn to detach from the emotional suffering it may cause, leading to better pain tolerance and improved quality of life (Ginexi et al., 2022).
- **Connects the default network:** As discussed previously, the default network is a group of brain regions that are active when your mind wanders. Mindfulness meditation strengthens the connection between this network and other parts of the brain responsible for focus and self-awareness. This improved communication can lead to better concentration, increased self-control, and a deeper understanding of your thoughts and emotions (Walton, 2015).
- **Combats high blood pressure:** By reducing stress, a major contributor to high blood pressure, meditation can help lower your blood pressure naturally. This can significantly improve cardiovascular health and reduce your risk of heart disease and stroke (Ginexi et al., 2022).
- **Leads to volume change in the brain:** Studies have shown that meditation can increase gray matter volume

in areas of the brain associated with learning, memory, and emotional regulation. This leads to improved cognitive function, which means that consistent meditation practices can literally reshape your brain in these positive ways (Walton, 2015).
- **Aids with insomnia and sleep quality:** If you struggle with a racing mind that keeps you up at night, meditation can be a game-changer. By quieting the mental chatter and promoting relaxation, meditation can help you fall asleep faster and experience deeper, more restful sleep. This can leave you feeling more energized and clear-headed throughout the day (Ginexi et al., 2022).

How to Meditate

It might sound challenging or even strange if you've never meditated before. Some people think of meditation as something that's not for them and "free-spirited" and assume it won't work for them. However, whether you're an art collector, CEO of a mega-corporation, or a second-grade teacher, you can use meditation and find it helpful. Give it a try right now, and follow along as I walk you through this meditation example:

1. Start by making yourself comfortable. Find a spot where you feel cozy and can sit comfortably without interruption.
2. Take a couple of deep breaths, in through your nose and out through your mouth. Soften your gaze and allow your eyes to close gently.
3. Become aware of your body as you continue to breathe. Notice your posture, the sensation of your body, and the position of your feet.

4. Tune in to your senses. What do you smell, hear, feel, or taste?
5. As you continue to breathe, turn your attention inward. Notice the areas of tension or discomfort. Notice them without judgment. Simply acknowledge how your body is feeling, then switch back to your thoughts.
6. What type of thoughts are you experiencing? Don't judge; simply observe as you bring your attention to your breathing once more. Take note of how your chest rises and falls. Count your breaths silently from one to ten. If your mind begins to wander, gently bring it back.
7. Continue to do so for as long as you like. Then, set your mind free. Allow your thoughts to go where they want as you follow them without judgment.
8. When you're ready to return, slowly become aware of your surroundings again. Then, open your eyes.
9. Celebrate your progress and notice how you are feeling more relaxed than before.

A key aspect of many meditation exercises is breathwork, which Chapter 4 delved into. Remember those steps on how to do it? Think of this as a beautiful fusion of the concepts explored in this mindfulness chapter. As you begin your meditation journey, remember to bring along the wisdom you've gained from those chapters. It's all about combining mindfulness with the power of your breath to find peace and presence in the here and now. The next chapter will look at the P of S-I-M-P-L-E as you discover progressive muscle relaxation.

7

PROGRESSIVE MUSCLE RELAXATION

HAVE you ever felt like you're carrying the weight of the world on your shoulders? Perhaps you feel like you're constantly in recovery mode, where your body is desperately trying to deal with the burden of the previous day. You're not alone. As you learned in earlier chapters, stress can manifest physically, and you often carry that stress in your muscles. You might not notice it at first, but over time, you'll begin to feel tense and sore, almost like you've just done an intense workout. That's why this strategy can help people overcome stress and let go of tension.

Progressive muscle relaxation is a technique that enables you to relax physically. In this chapter, you'll discover exactly what it is, its benefits, and how you can implement this technique at home. Let's get started and release all that pent-up tension in your body.

What Is Progressive Muscle Relaxation?

When you're stressed and overwhelmed, your muscles become tense. Imagine a coiled spring that gets increasingly tense as the weight piles up. Progressive muscle relaxation (PMR) supports the coiled spring, allowing your muscles to release all the tension. PMR can work both as a quick fix and a long-term solution to deal with the tightness and stress.

PMR was developed based on the idea that when you are physically relaxed, your mind will follow. It guides you through steps where you systematically tense and release different muscle groups. As you breathe in, you will tense a specific muscle group, and with the exhale, you will release all the tension, allowing you to relax completely. This action gets repeated multiple times until all the muscles in your body are relaxed.

Many professionals, such as therapists and psychologists, use PMR, and although it has gained popularity over the last decade, it's not a new technique. PMR has been around for over a century and started with Edmund Jacobson, a student at Harvard who was fascinated with anxiety after experiencing childhood trauma. At Harvard, he began researching different techniques, including PMR, which has since been refined for modern use (Sutton, 2018). PMR focuses on recognizing the connection between the mind and the body, promoting overall well-being.

Benefits of Progressive Muscle Relaxation

PMR offers a whole host of benefits that can improve your physical and mental well-being. Not only does it bring about a deep sense of relaxation, but it also teaches you to recognize the difference between a tense and a relaxed muscle. This can be a game changer when it comes to managing stress, as identifying the physical symptoms of tension allows you to take appropriate steps to release the stress before it becomes a problem.

PMR has also been shown to contribute to overall health, as it can manage insomnia and high blood pressure. Because of this, many medical practitioners offer PMR to their patients as part of their treatment plans (Mackereth & Tomlinson, 2010). These benefits also trickle into the realm of sport, where the mind and body are closely intertwined. Athletes use PMR to improve their sleep, but it also helps manage their pain (McCloughan et al., 2016).

As if these benefits aren't enough, PMR is also used to help cancer patients who are undergoing chemotherapy. It's well known that chemotherapy can take a brutal toll on a patient's quality of life, and PMR has been shown to alleviate symptoms caused by chemotherapy, including nausea, pain, anxiety, and depression. On top of that, PMR can also improve mood swings and help prevent headaches when faced with a stressful situation (Charalambous et al., 2016).

It's clear that PMR isn't simply a relaxation technique but a versatile tool that can improve your health, enhance your performance, and help you navigate life's challenges. Up next, let's take a look at how you can make use of PMR in your day-to-day life.

How Do You Do Progressive Muscle Relaxation?

The best part about PMR is that it can be easily practiced at home. It requires nothing more than your focus and attention and a quiet space free from distractions. The key is to tense each muscle for at least 5 seconds while inhaling. Then, as you exhale, fully relax those muscles for 10–20 seconds before moving on to the next group. Why don't you give it a try right now?

1. Start by finding a quiet space to sit or lie down, depending on your preference. Take five deep, slow breaths as you prepare yourself for the practice.
2. Curl your toes tightly toward you, feeling the tension in your feet. Hold for at least five seconds, then slowly release and wiggle your toes.
3. Next, point your toes downward to flex your calves and hold for 5 seconds. Relax and let your feet flop loosely.

Bring your knees toward each other, hold, and release, following the 5-second hold and 15-second release format.
4. Focus your attention on your thighs next. Squeeze your thigh muscles as if trying to push your heels together. Hold for 5 seconds, then release and feel the tension drain away. Don't forget to breathe as you continue with the muscle relaxation technique.
5. Next, clench your buttocks tightly and release; feel them sink back down. Bring the tension to your abdomen as you tighten your stomach as if bracing for a punch. Hold for 5 seconds and release.
6. Take a deep breath and hold your chest tightly—release as you exhale completely. Shrug your shoulders toward your ears, feeling the tension in your neck and shoulders. Remember to breathe even when you're clenching the muscles. Hold for 5 seconds and release for 15.
7. Next, focus on your arms and hands by making a tight fist. Keep it squeezed for 5 seconds, and then open your hand and let the tension flow out of your arms.
8. Gently turn your head to one side, bringing your ear toward your shoulder. Hold for 5 seconds, release the tension, and then repeat on the other side. Let your head return to the center and feel your neck muscles relax.
9. Lastly, focus on your facial muscles. Scrunch up your face as tightly as you can. Hold for 5 seconds, then relax and let your face go slack.

After you've completed the technique, check in with yourself to see how you're feeling. Are you feeling calmer and more at peace? If you still feel some stress, repeat the process and remember to continuously breathe as you work through it.

Incorporating Progressive Muscle Relaxation Into Your Daily Life

Your day is most likely already filled with hundreds of tasks and responsibilities you feel you *must* do, and PMR doesn't have to add to that daunting list. A traditional 20-minute session may seem time-intensive, so why not adapt it a little? Remember, PMR was created to help you release stress, not add more tension to your day. If you have limited time, you can shorten the hold and release periods as long as the release is longer than the hold. You can also choose to break the session up into smaller bits. For example, plan to do half of it in the morning before you get dressed and the second half before bed at night after the rest of the family is already in bed. Whatever works for your schedule is the right way to do it.

Many audio and video recordings are available for PMR practice, which offer guided relaxation sessions. If that sounds like your cup of tea, give it a go. You can also look for PMR apps that provide a wide range of exercises of various lengths, making it easier for you to adjust the timings based on your schedule each day.

By making time for PMR in your daily life, you can experience the benefits of relaxation wherever you go. Whether you have a few minutes or a more extended period, resources are available to support your journey toward greater calmness and tranquility. Remember, PMR is a fantastic tool for managing stress both in the short and long term, so don't underestimate its power.

The next chapter explores the L of S-I-M-P-L-E: laughter. Get ready to work those core muscles with some good, old-fashioned giggles.

8

LAUGHTER

The human race has one really effective weapon, and that is laughter.

- MARK TWAIN

HAVE you ever wondered why those funny cat videos you watch after a rough day instantly lift your mood? Is it because of your love for cats? Or, perhaps because those cute, cuddly creatures distract you from the stress? What if I told you that the key is actually laughter? As cliché as it might sound, laughter is often the best medicine, and a little bit more every day might just be what the doctor prescribed to overcome your stress. Laughter is more than just temporary relief. It is a powerful tool that you can use to combat stress and anxiety.

This chapter will explore what laughter is, its incredible health benefits, and easy ways to incorporate more laughter into your day-to-day life. So, get ready for some chuckles as you laugh away your stress.

Laughter Is the Best Medicine

When I was a little girl, I was admitted to the hospital and had to stay there for an entire week. Every day, my dad would show up and turn on the TV. He would take me into his loving arms, and together, we watched his favorite sitcom, *Friends*. Back then, I thought it was his way of keeping me entertained and keeping himself from getting too bored. But as I got older, I learned that there was much more to it. He understood the power of laughter, and I'm convinced that laughing every day heavily contributed to my good mood and quick recovery. I remember the rest of my family commenting on my good spirits and positive attitude, and I now know why my dad did what he did.

My dad wasn't the only one who cracked the code, though. Laughter therapy, which is basically just fancy lingo for laughing on purpose, has been hailed as one of the best non-pharmacological interventions out there. It's a universal remedy for stress and anxiety that's been around for a long time. Ancient cultures have long recognized the profound impact of laughter on our mental, physical, and social health (Akimbekov & Razzaque, 2021). Today, we have science to back it up.

Studies have shown that laughter can do wonders for your brain chemistry. When you laugh, your brain releases feel-good neurotransmitters like dopamine and serotonin, which can lift your mood and help you feel more relaxed (Yim, 2016). Through laughter, you suppress the bioactivities of epinephrine, cortisol, and dihydroxyphenylacetic acid, which are hormones that contribute to stress, anxiety, and depression. In other words, when you laugh and boost your serotonin and dopamine hormones, you actively decrease the risks of anxiety, depression, and stress.

Laughter has the ability to lift your mood. Have you ever felt grumpy, but after laughing at your friend's silly joke, you suddenly feel much better? Well, that's the power of laughter. Laughter also changes your physical body. It loosens tense muscles and keeps your heart healthy. On top of that, laughter can be used as a natural painkiller and can decrease pain triggered by chemicals in your body. Let's look at these benefits in more detail in a moment. Since your mind and your body are closely connected, it comes as no surprise to learn that when you laugh, you achieve benefits for both (Yim, 2016).

Why don't you try it? It might feel silly, but challenge yourself to laugh right now. Don't hold back. Let out a hearty laugh and allow those feel-good hormones to rush through your body. After a proper laughing session, evaluate how you're feeling. Who knows, perhaps that slight annoyance you might have been feeling has disappeared altogether.

Laughter and Stress

A friend of mine recently shared her own childhood hospital story with me, and although she didn't watch *Friends* every day, she found a way to laugh. How? With the help of the hospital clown, she laughed and kept her spirits high throughout her stay, and she recalled that memory as one of her favorite childhood memories. Hospital clowns might sound like something from a Stephen King novel, but they are incredibly beneficial and can aid in the recovery of young and old. Hospital clowns reduce anxiety and stress for both the children and their parents. My friend shared with me how the hospital clown made her a balloon chicken, which she could wear on her head like a hat, and how he made a flower for her mom, making them both smile.

By recognizing the power of laughter and its ability to reduce stress, some hospitals have created Clown Care Units, where clowns help people laugh and release anxiety while in the hospital or awaiting results. While laughing at a clown might seem like the obvious thing to do, how can you implement this at home? It's not so easy to crack a smile when you're knee-deep in stress, drowning in deadlines, and don't have access to a clown at all times of the day.

Research has shown that laughter isn't just a momentary distraction but a powerful stress-buster, so you need to find ways to make yourself laugh when you need it, not just when you feel like it (Akimbekov & Razzaque, 2021). Something as silly as watching a funny video on your phone can significantly decrease your stress. So, instead of biting your nails or pulling out your hair from the stress, turn to YouTube and search for some funny videos. No matter what stress you're dealing with, a little bit of laughter can be the perfect remedy.

By choosing to laugh, you actively embrace its power to combat stress and anxiety. That's why many therapists and psychologists incorporate laughter therapy into their counseling sessions when finding ways to help their clients manage stress. The key lies in choosing to laugh even when you're not in the mood to laugh. A "fake it till you make it" approach is encouraged when it comes to using laughter to combat stress. It turns out that your body doesn't always know the difference between real and fake laughter, so you'll reap the benefits even if you're faking them at first (Louie et al., 2016). Let's take a look at both the short and long-term benefits of laughter before looking at specific ways to incorporate laughter into your day-to-day life.

Short-Term Benefits of Laughter

A previous chapter discussed how stress can cause relationships to suffer. Well, good news: Laughter can be just the solution you need! Laughter can bring people together like very few other things in this world. Take a moment to think about the last time you laughed so hard your stomach started to hurt, and you thought it would never stop. Who were you with, and how did you feel toward that person afterward? Chances are, you felt much closer, and that's because laughter creates bonds.

The best part about laughter is that it's good not only for your relationships but also for your mind and body. After a good laugh, you might notice that your muscles feel loose and relaxed. That's because laughter helps your body to chill, reducing muscle tension and lowering your heart rate (Dunbar et al., 2011). Studies have also shown that laughter can act as a natural painkiller. It enables you to tolerate pain better by triggering the release of pain-relieving chemicals in the body (Lapierre et al., 2019).

When you laugh, you release endorphins, one of your body's feel-good hormones. With endorphins rushing through your body, you'll feel that warm, fuzzy feeling we all cherish and love, making even that nasty customer slightly more bearable. Laughter isn't just there to rev you up but to help you remain calm under pressure. After a good laugh, you'll feel relaxed, motivated, and collected.

I heard a story about a couple who used to argue over everything in their relationship. One day, someone advised them to lie on the ground on their stomachs as soon as they started arguing. They decided to try the advice and found that it was impossible to remain angry and defensive over small things when you were lying on the ground with your partner, facing the floor. Instead, they started laughing and quickly realized that they were arguing over unimportant matters. By laughing together, the couple grew closer to one another and stopped arguing over all the little things.

Long-Term Benefits of Laughter

Now that you better understand the short-term benefits of laughter, it's time to expand your horizons and look into the future. Is laughter helpful for your future self, or is it something you benefit from only in that particular moment? Luckily, laughter is greatly beneficial in both the short and long term.

The first long-term benefit is that it boosts your immune system. When you're laughing, your body releases neuropeptides, which remove stress and boost your immune response. This can enhance your ability to fight disease and remain strong and healthy. Additionally, laughter also benefits the heart. When you're laughing, you're basically having a short cardio workout. Benefiting both your heart vessels and increasing the blood flow, laughter aids in your physical heart health, decreasing the chances of heart disease.

Speaking of a workout, laughter can also burn some serious calories. While it's not a substitute for the gym, it does provide an additional calorie burn, prompting your metabolism to work harder. While losing a few extra pounds thanks to laughing is great, research has also shown that laughter can add more years to your life, especially in cancer patients (Robinson et al., 2018).

While laughter can bring immediate relief from stress, it can also improve your mental health in the long term. So, keep laughing, even when you're not in the mood.

Incorporating Laughter Into Your Day-To-Day Life

Now that you know laughter is important and helpful, you might notice that your funny bone needs a little workout. Where do you even begin in your attempt to invoke purposeful laughter? Here are six ways to incorporate laughter into your day-to-day life.

Laughter Yoga

If you're looking to add more laughter to your day, laughter yoga offers a unique approach. It combines elements of yoga breathing and playful exercises to get you laughing, even if you don't feel like it at first. The idea is to engage in simulated laughter exercises, clapping, making eye contact, and laughing together in a group setting. The exciting thing is that even though the laughter might start out feeling a bit forced, it can lead to real laughter. The best part? Laughter yoga is open to everyone, regardless of yoga experience or comedic taste. You can find classes online or in your community, but there's also no need for a formal group setting. Simply search for "laughter yoga exercises" online and find some simple routines to practice at home. Remember, even if the laughter starts out feeling a bit silly, your body will still react by releasing those feel-good chemicals.

Funny Content

Another way to add more laughter to your life is by consuming funny content. There's certainly no shortcoming of stressful or downright depressive content out there. So, when your goal is to add more laughter to your day, follow content creators who make you laugh or put on a funny movie. You can also focus on watching humorous TV shows instead of something dark and serious. There are also many great, hilarious podcasts you can try, so try to incorporate more of those into your daily life.

Laugh at Yourself

Finding humor in your own mishaps can be a powerful way to infuse your day with laughter. We all make mistakes, have silly moments, and sometimes even trip over thin air. Instead of dwelling on the embarrassment, try flipping the script and seeing the humor in the situation. Imagine yourself as a character in a sitcom, fumbling through life's little challenges. Did you burn your toast for breakfast again? Picture it as a perfectly timed gag. Spilled coffee on your shirt? Channel your inner comedian and quip about your newfound tie-dye look. Laughing at yourself doesn't mean belittling yourself but acknowledging the absurdity of everyday situations and finding the funny side.

Laughter Exercise

Laughter exercises are a fantastic way to inject those chuckles into your day. Find a quiet spot and set a timer for a few minutes. Start by taking some deep breaths, releasing any tension with each exhale. Then, choose a playful activity: maybe some exaggerated fake yawning, energetic silent giggling, or even pretending to laugh at a silly joke. The key is to act it out with full commitment, even if it initially feels strange. Focus on the physical sensations of laughter: the crinkling of your eyes, the movement of your diaphragm. After a few minutes, stop and notice how you feel. Chances are, you'll find yourself feeling lighter and more relaxed, with a smile lingering on your face. Laughter exercises are a convenient and effective way to bring a dose of joy into your daily routine.

Laughter as Part of Your Routine

You can make laughter a part of your daily routine by thinking about what brings you genuine joy. Do you have a friend who always cracks you up with their witty banter? Schedule a call or meet up for coffee. Board game nights with friends or family can also be a goldmine for giggles. Choose a game that encourages lighthearted competition and silliness, like Charades or Pictionary. The key is to find activities that spark joy and laughter, whether it's through social interaction or simply indulging in some lighthearted entertainment. By making these fun activities a regular part of your routine, you'll incorporate laughter into your day in a natural and enjoyable way.

Smile More

Smiling leads to laughter, so if you want to laugh more, start by smiling more. You can smile more by changing a few small things in your daily routine. Look up from your phone and share a smile with people on the street, or smile at the barista making your coffee. You can even smile at your elevator companions. You might be surprised by the positive ripple effect, as a smile can be a simple act that sparks joy in yourself and others.

With these simple ways, you can add more laughter to your day-to-day life and transform even the darkest day into one that feels warm and sunny. By laughing more, you'll soon reap the benefits and feel more relaxed. The next chapter explores the final letter of S-I-M-P-L-E: exercise. So, tie your laces and get ready to get active.

9

EXERCISE

You know that feeling after a good workout when you're sweaty but smiling, like you can accomplish anything? That's the power of exercise, my friend. Exercise has a way of making you feel strong and empowered, and that's because it's got more to it than just the physical aspect. Exercise isn't only about getting fit; it's about feeling good inside and out. In fact, exercise is one of the most effective ways to combat stress and anxiety.

This chapter will explore how breaking a sweat can help reduce stress and why exercise and movement are so beneficial. You'll also discover the various types of exercises you can try to combat stress. Don't worry; you don't have to be a gym rat to reap the benefits of exercise. You can choose many exercises; you just have to find the right fit for you. The chapter ends by exploring ways to add movement to your daily routine. So, grab your sneakers, and let's get moving!

Exercising and Stress

Let's start by discussing the connection between exercise and stress relief. You know those days when stress feels like it's piling up faster than you can handle? Everyone has been there. But did you know that regular exercise can be your secret against stress and its nasty effects? Exercise might be marketed as hitting the gym daily to look a certain way or aim for a certain weight, but it's so much more than that.

Exercise and movement can greatly aid in managing stress and anxiety. It doesn't matter what type of exercise you enjoy or are into; it facilitates a mental and physical release of stress. In other words, whether you want to hit the gym every day and be as strong as possible or simply enjoy a leisurely stroll through nature, it will help to decrease your stress and improve your mental and physical well-being. It also doesn't have to feel like you're punishing your body. In fact, by viewing exercise as the act of simply moving your body instead of another thing on your to-do list, you'll reap even more benefits.

Moving your body consistently will help calm your mind and distract you from your worries, regardless of the exercise that you choose. At the end of the day, you need to find an exercise that you enjoy since you'll be more likely to stick with it when it's something that brings you instant joy. So, as you look deeper into the benefits of exercise, remember that you can access all of these benefits with any movement you want to incorporate. Whether you're hitting the trails, flowing through a yoga class, or simply taking a leisurely stroll around the block, exercise might just be an essential tool in managing your stress.

Benefits of Exercise

Now that you know that it's recommended to incorporate exercise to manage stress, you can also look at the other benefits of exercise. Let's start by exploring the science behind why exercise can help reduce stress.

Reduces Stress

When you hit the pavement for a run, dive into a swim, or power through a cardio session, your body responds in all sorts of fascinating ways. Exercise helps dial down the levels of stress hormones like adrenaline and cortisol while cranking up the production of feel-good chemicals like norepinephrine, serotonin, and dopamine. It gives your body a boost of endorphins, which help reduce pain and give you that post-workout high (Greenberg, 2017). When you're focused on your body's movements during a workout, you tend to forget about all the little annoyances and stresses of the day. It's like hitting the reset button for your brain, leaving you feeling calm, clear-headed, and better equipped to take on whatever comes your way.

Improves Resilience

The second benefit to explore is that exercise can build resilience. Regular aerobic exercise, like brisk walking or cycling, can make you more resilient to stress in the long run as it strengthens your body, boosts your energy levels, and helps you maintain a healthy weight. All of these elements can help you feel more confident and capable when life throws you a curveball (Greenberg, 2017). It's like a workout for your stress response system, helping your body practice dealing with those fight, flight, or freeze situations and protecting your cardiovascular, digestive, and immune systems from the harmful effects of stress. Exercise can also help you to remain more positive during stressful situations (Childs & de Wit, 2014).

Boosts Cognitive Function

Another benefit of exercise is that it can boost cognitive function. Exercise works as a brain booster, and studies have shown that vigorous exercise can help protect your brain from premature aging caused by chronic stress (Puterman et al., 2010). When you're out there breaking a sweat, you're not only getting fitter—you're also giving your brain a serious upgrade. In addition, exercise helps prevent ruminating by altering blood flow to areas of the brain involved in repeatedly bringing up stressful thoughts. Researchers have found that even a 10-minute exercise break during a stressful exam week can lower stress levels and improve cognitive function (Shaw & Lubetzky, 2021). Intense workouts and recreational exercise can engage you in a way that distracts you from stress and gets you outdoors to enjoy the sunshine and appreciate the beauty of nature.

Improves Mood

Lastly, exercise can significantly benefit your mood and act as a happiness booster for your brain. During exercise, the production of feel-good chemicals called endorphins are pumped up, giving you that "on top of the world" feeling, also referred to as the runner's high. Whether you're hitting the tennis court, hiking in nature, or just dancing around your living room, any aerobic activity can give you that same mood boost. As it boosts your mood, exercise also increases your self-confidence and can lower symptoms of mild depression and anxiety. Overall, it can turn your frown upside down.

No matter what exercise and movement you're getting into, remember that it's about more than just physical health. It's about equipping your body and mind with tools to improve stress management and resilience. Now that you understand the benefits, it's time to explore a few types of exercise that you might want to try.

Aerobic Exercise

Aerobic exercises are any type of exercise that gets your heart rate up and keeps it up for a sustained period. This increases your breathing rate and makes your body use more oxygen. On the other hand, anaerobic exercises are movements that require less oxygen, such as strength training and weight lifting. Overall, aerobic exercise is essential for your health and fitness, as it can help to

- increase cardiovascular health.
- strengthen your heart and lungs.
- improve blood circulation.
- reduce your risk of heart disease, stroke, and type 2 diabetes.
- help you maintain a healthy weight.
- elevate your mood and reduce stress.

There are many different types of aerobic exercises, so you can find one that you enjoy and that fits into your lifestyle. Some popular options include brisk walking, running, swimming, cycling, dancing, and elliptical training. However, aerobic exercise isn't only about getting your heart pumping and your lungs working; it's also about giving your head a workout. Regular aerobic exercise has the amazing ability to not only exhilarate but also relax you. It counteracts feelings of depression and dissipates stress. As you start to see changes in your body, your self-image will also get a boost, and you'll begin to feel more confident. This confidence will spill into other areas of your life, helping you tackle challenges with renewed vigor and determination.

Yoga and Pilates

Seeing yoga and Pilates in everyone's morning routine videos online has probably got you wondering why everyone is doing it and how to get started. Yoga and Pilates are more than just striking poses or contorting your body in different shapes. These practices are all about connecting your body and mind, finding balance, and kicking stress to the curb.

As I mentioned in Chapter 6, there was a time in my life when I was really stressed. Due to all the stress, I suffered from intense migraines, and one month in particular was incredibly difficult. It was around that time I decided to start yoga, and thanks to my daily sessions, I felt something amazing happen within the first month. I only got one migraine the whole month. For someone who used to be sidelined by migraines on the regular, that was a game-changer. It's like my body finally found its rhythm again, and I felt physically healthy enough in the day to work toward my goals.

Yoga practices date back many, many years and were first described by Patanjali, the founder of Pilates (Woodyard, 2011). Yoga and Pilates are both mind-body exercise practices that offer a powerful combination of physical movement, breathwork, and mental focus. Yoga incorporates postures (known as asanas in Sanskrit) designed to improve flexibility and strength, while Pilates emphasizes core engagement and controlled movements for building core stability and improving posture. Both practices integrate focused breathing techniques, encouraging deep inhales and exhales to calm the nervous system and promote relaxation.

This unique blend of physical and mental elements makes them perfect for stress reduction. The physical movements in yoga and Pilates help release muscle tension that often builds up during stressful periods. Focused breathing techniques further activate the body's relaxation response, lowering stress hormones and promoting feelings of calmness. Additionally, the present-moment awareness cultivated in both practices allows you to temporarily detach from worries and anxieties, offering a mental break from daily stressors. By incorporating yoga or Pilates into your routine, you gain valuable tools to manage stress effectively and cultivate a sense of overall well-being.

The beauty of yoga and Pilates is that they don't have to take a lot of time out of your day. You can complete a workout in as little as 15 minutes and reap the benefits.

The different yoga movements help to release muscle knots and stress, as well as other emotions, while also releasing endorphins. This means you're getting a physical workout and a mood boost (Cronkleton, 2021). When you're on your mat, flowing through those poses, you actively combat stress as you become more aware of your present moment. Studies have shown that women who practice yoga three times a week for four weeks experience a significant reduction in stress, depression, and anxiety (Azami et al., 2018). Similarly, men who practice yoga will experience reduced cortisol levels (Eda et al., 2020).

To get started, here are a couple of yoga poses you can try to incorporate yoga into your daily routine.

Cat-Cow Pose (Marjaryasana to Bitilasana)

1. Start on all fours with your wrists under your shoulders and knees under your hips. This is known as the tabletop position.
2. Inhale as you arch your back and gaze upward (cow pose), and exhale as you round your spine and tuck your chin (cat pose).
3. Flow between these positions for about a minute, syncing your breath with your movements.

Child's Pose (Balasana)

1. From a kneeling position, sit on the top of your foot and fold forward, resting your forehead on the mat.
2. Extend your arms in front of you or alongside your legs.
3. Take deep breaths and focus on releasing tension.
4. You can use a cushion for extra support under your forehead, torso, or thighs.
5. Hold this pose for up to 5 minutes.

Legs-Up-The-Wall Pose (Viparita Karani)

1. Sit close to a wall and lie on your back, placing your legs up the wall with straight knees.
2. Your hips can be positioned next to the wall or a few inches away.
3. Keep your arms alongside your body or place one hand on your belly and the other on your chest.
4. Relax deeply into this pose, allowing for improved circulation and lymph flow.
5. Hold it for as long as you have time; 15 minutes is ideal.

Corpse Pose (Savasana)

1. Lie flat on your back with your feet slightly wider than your hips and your toes turning outward.
2. Position your arms at a 45-degree angle from your body.
3. Close your eyes and focus on breathing deeply, allowing your entire body to relax completely.
4. Stay in this pose for as long as you have time; 10–20

minutes being the ideal time. Embrace the calmness and tranquility that this movement brings.

Building Exercise Into Your Routine

You might run into a few barriers when adding exercise to your daily routine. It's not easy to make exercise a habit, but that doesn't mean it's impossible. Let's address some of these barriers and explore how to overcome them effectively. The first and the biggest obstacle is time. Everyone leads busy lives, and it can feel like there's just no room in the day for a workout. But here's the thing: Even a few minutes of exercise can make a difference. Instead of aiming for long gym sessions, incorporate short bursts of activity throughout your day. Take the stairs instead of the elevator, go for a brisk walk during your lunch break, or do a quick bodyweight workout before bed. Every little bit counts!

Another common barrier is knowledge. It can be intimidating to step into a gym or start a new exercise routine when you're unsure what you're doing. But there are plenty of resources out there to help you get started. You can find workout videos online, join a fitness class, or even hire a personal trainer for guidance. Remember, everyone has to start somewhere—don't be afraid to ask for help if you need it. One of the best ways to overcome this barrier and the barrier of feeling insecure is to ask a friend to join you on your fitness journey. By having a buddy, you'll also be more likely to be consistent, as you'll have someone to keep you accountable.

Another barrier is losing motivation after a couple of days or weeks. The best way to combat this is by making exercise a habit and creating SMART goals for your fitness journey. SMART goals are goals that are specific, measurable, attainable, relevant, and timely, and by creating SMART goals, you'll be sure to stay encouraged and motivated as you achieve your smaller milestones. For example, a SMART goal might look something like this: "I will spend 30 minutes walking around my neighborhood three times a week for the next two months to improve my fitness."

If you're struggling to make exercise a regular habit, you might find some helpful tips in the book *Atomic Habits* by James Clear. Clear breaks down the science of habit formation and offers practical strategies for building new habits.

Remember, exercise is a potent antidote to stress in your daily life. From aerobic activities like walking to the calming practices of yoga and Pilates, physical movement offers both immediate relief and long-term benefits for stress management. Whether it's dedicating 15 minutes a day or embracing a more extensive routine, the positive impact on your physical and mental well-being is undeniable.

Now that you know all the strategies of the S-I-M-P-L-E framework, the next few chapters go into some concepts that can complement or supplement the framework, starting with visualization.

10

VISUALIZATION

You might have heard of speaking things into existence, but have you ever considered visualizing something into existence? That's something I've experienced personally throughout my life. Visualization is like a superpower hiding in plain sight, waiting for us to tap into its potential. My journey with visualization began quite unexpectedly at the age of eleven. Instead of starting high school like my peers, I found myself confined to a hospital bed. During this challenging time, my dad introduced me to the concept of visualization, although I didn't realize it at the time.

Every day, my dad would encourage me to close my eyes and vividly imagine walking through the doors of the school, chatting with friends, and sitting in class. So, I did. Day after day, I immersed myself in those imagined scenes with unwavering focus. Despite the doctors' initial prognosis, I found myself walking through those school doors sooner than anyone expected. It was then that I realized the incredible influence of thoughts and mental imagery on reality.

Since then, I've continued to harness the power of visualization in various aspects of my life. From picturing myself passing my driving test to envisioning the promotion I wanted, visualization has become an effective strategy for transforming stressful situations into more manageable ones. It's like amplifying your dreams and making them a reality by using visual imagery. This chapter will explore the concept of visualization and dive into what it is, why it's beneficial, and the different techniques of visualization you can adopt into your daily life. Get ready to imagine the stress-free world you want to live in!

What Is Visualization?

Visualizing success isn't just a tool for daydreamers; it's a scientifically backed technique used in various forms of therapy and self-improvement. While many people dismiss visualization as being all about zoning out and imagining themselves on a sunny beach, it's actually a powerful technique for calming your mind and body. Professionals also use visualization therapy to treat anxiety, depression, and chronic stress. A study conducted found that participants who use visualization are more likely to overcome stress and have reduced symptoms of depression and anxiety (Rees, 1995). That's because visualization enables you to picture your desired outcome, allowing you to feel it and fully immerse yourself in the possibility of success.

Why is that helpful for our realities? Because it trains the mind to believe in your potential and your goals. The mind is like a muscle; the more you train it, the stronger it will grow. By repeating visualizations, your brain will begin to blur the lines between imagination and reality, boosting your confidence and motivation to tackle the obstacles ahead.

Elite athletes often use visualization to mentally prepare for competitions. They envision every detail, from start to finish. That means they also simulate worst-case scenarios and prepare themselves for how they will handle that situation if it happens in real life. It's almost like they are giving their brains a trial run, so when the big moment arrives, they're ready for whatever might come their way.

However, visualization isn't exclusive to pro athletes and professionals. You and I can use it in our everyday lives. Here are a few tips and tricks to keep in mind when starting your visualization journey:

- First off, practice makes perfect. When you first start, it might feel a bit awkward, but the more you engage in the exercise, the easier it gets. Make it a daily habit, and eventually, it'll feel like second nature.
- Another tip is to not only focus on what you see. Engage all your senses. Imagine the sound of birds chirping as you walk through the forest, the smell of the pine trees in the air, and the dense woodland floor crunching under your feet. The more vivid you make it, the more effective it'll be.
- Finally, don't shy away from stressful thoughts. Instead, have a plan to deal with them. Visualize them melting away or being replaced with something positive. It's all about turning those negative thoughts into something you can let go of.

Benefits of Visualization

Now that you know what visualization is, let's pull back the curtain and explore how it really works and why it's beneficial. Over the last decade, many scientists have been researching the power of the mind and the influence of imagination on reality, and the findings are fascinating. According to Tori Wager, who heads up the Cognitive and Affective Neuroscience Lab over at the University of Colorado Boulder, your imagination has a pretty big impact on your brain and body, affecting your overall well-being (Marshall, 2018). It's not just a fun way to distract yourself but can positively influence your mind and body.

Using brain-imaging studies, researchers have found that when you imagine things, a part of your mind believes you're actually doing it (Lohr, 2015). In other words, the lines between reality and fiction begin to blur into one, preparing you mentally and physically for what's to come. This mental practice can help you improve specific activities, like recovering from an injury or nailing a dance routine. It can also be used to overcome fears and phobias or to prepare yourself for a difficult conversation. When you visualize something, your brain activity increases, and it triggers the parts of your brain responsible for managing emotions, understanding others, and being creative (Velikova & Nordtug, 2018).

Visualization has also been shown to improve your mood and outlook on life. People who visualize often are more likely to remain optimistic when things get hard (Murphy et al., 2015). Visualization can also help you make better decisions and prepare for possible obstacles. In other words, it helps you to avoid and, if needed, solve problems before they occur (Davis, 2023). Now that you understand the benefits, let's explore visualization techniques.

Techniques for Visualization

There are many visualization techniques you can choose from, and it's all about experimenting and finding the one that works best for you. Before getting started, here's an outline of how to approach any visualization technique:

1. Find your space: Before you begin your visualization exercise, find a relaxing space. That includes a mental and physical space of safety. Physically, this might mean finding a quiet, cozy place where you won't be interrupted. Mentally, it might mean imagining a beautiful meadow with wild horses or an island holiday. Whatever makes you feel relaxed and peaceful, both physically and mentally, is the place you'll begin.

2. Begin to dream: Once you're cozy and comfortable, close your eyes and begin to immerse yourself in your safe bubble. Look around and notice what you see, smell, hear, or even taste. Pay attention to the small details as you totally transport yourself into your relaxing world.
3. Release the tension: Take a few deep breaths, and as you exhale, let go of the tension in your body. Relax your shoulders, unclench your jaw, and breathe out everything causing you stress. When a stressful thought pops up, gently bring your thoughts back to your relaxed space.

By starting with these three steps, any of the visualization techniques will be beneficial and more likely to grant you the peace and calm you've been looking for. Let's take a look at some visualization techniques that you can try.

Blue Light Visualization

When you feel stressed or overwhelmed with anxiety, blue light visualization can help you to calm down, let go of stress, and embrace a new perspective.

1. Start by closing your eyes and imagine a large blue orb illuminating a dark room.
2. The blue light comes closer to you and hovers over your head. Breathe in the light, allowing it to fill every inch of your body.
3. As the light fills you up, you see the tension and the stress disappear. There isn't space for both the blue light and the anxiety, so imagine being filled with the light to the brim, leaving no inch of your body without it.
4. With each breath, allow yourself to experience the peace

and calm of the blue light until it leaves you totally immersed and filled with peace (Davidson, 2018).

Goal Visualization

Goal visualization is the technique you use when you want to achieve a very specific goal. This is the type of visualization athletes often use, but you can use it to focus on other goals as well, no matter how big or small.

1. Start by closing your eyes, taking a few deep breaths, and imagine reaching your goal.
2. For example, if you're anxious before an important interview, imagine yourself walking into the room with confidence, answering all the questions, and charming them completely. By the end of the interview, they will offer you the job, and it's better than you expected.
3. As you visualize success, let go of the stress and anxieties and trust that you are prepared for a positive outcome (Star, 2022).

Color Breathing

Color breathing is an excellent technique for relieving stress and improving your general mood.

1. Start by thinking of something you want to embrace, either an emotion or any positive feeling.
2. Next, assign a specific color to that feeling or emotion. Once you have assigned a color, close your eyes and visualize the color you chose.
3. As you inhale, imagine that color washing all over you from head to toe. With every exhale, pull the color even

closer to you until your entire body is covered in that color.
4. Imagine the color drowning out any other negative feelings and embrace the lightness that this new color is providing you (Legg, 2020).

Loving Kindness Visualization

This visualization fosters a feeling of compassion toward yourself and others and can be incredibly helpful in dealing with the causes of your current stress.

1. Start with the usual set-up, finding a comfortable space and breathing deeply.
2. Next, imagine the person you want to show kindness to. Think about how you're currently feeling toward this person.
3. Imagine a hardship they might be dealing with right now and allow that hardship to change your perspective. Focus on the positive emotions you want to give them, such as peace, joy, and healing.
4. Picture these positive feelings as a golden light spreads from your heart to theirs. Say something positive about the person and watch as they fill with positive light.
5. As you exhale, let go of any negativity or animosity you might still carry (Legg, 2020).

Closed Window Visualization

Anxious thoughts and stress can often feel like people shouting at you. Whether you've had a rough day at work or are ruminating over something a family member said, it can feel overwhelming as the noise of the day follows you around. This technique can help you to shut out the negativity and stress of the day.

1. Start by closing your eyes and taking a few deep breaths. Imagine a large window, and right outside the window, people are screaming and talking loudly, representing the negativity and stress of the day.
2. Now, imagine yourself closing the window firmly. As you do, all the noise stops and is drowned out by the solid barrier of the window.
3. Now that the noise is gone, accept it and walk away from the window, leaving the loud voices behind (Davidson, 2018).

You can try out these techniques in your own time, but I also want to walk you through one more technique, known as guided imagery. Don't worry; all you have to do is sit back and follow my voice.

Guided Imagery

Guided imagery is when you allow someone else to create the visualization for you and follow their lead. As you listen to what the other person says, you can follow along in your mind, creating a world that fits with the image they're describing. That way, you don't have to focus on imagining anything other than what you're being guided to. A study found that patients who listened to guided imagery before their surgery were less likely to experience stress associated with further complications. They also experienced less pain than those who didn't listen to the guided imagery (Tusek et al., 1997). In other words, it has solid backing behind it. Let's try it right now as I walk you through your very own guided imagery:

1. First, prepare yourself by finding a comfortable space and taking a couple of deep breaths. Close your eyes and allow yourself to drift into a state of relaxation.
2. Now, begin to picture yourself standing in a rainforest. You're surrounded by luscious greenery and bright plants. You feel completely safe.
3. Begin to notice the sounds around you. You hear the birds chirping and the wind rustling through the trees. You feel the warmth of the sun on your skin as you walk through the forest.
4. You follow the beautiful path, which leads you to a clearing where there's a waterfall and light dancing through the clouds. You smell the fresh air as you walk closer to the water. You dip your toes and feel peace rush over you.
5. Take a moment to really immerse yourself in this scene and let go of any tension or stress. When you're ready, slowly open your eyes.
6. Take a moment to appreciate the peace and calm you just experienced.

If you enjoyed this guided imagery and want to explore more, you can find similar sessions on YouTube or apps dedicated to visualization. Remember, it's all about finding the one that works for you, so don't be scared to try out a few.

Now that you've explored visualization as a stress-release strategy, only one remains. The next chapter will examine the power of routine and explore why you can benefit from it.

11

THE POWER OF ROUTINE

LIFE CAN BE OVERWHELMING SOMETIMES. Between work, school, family, friends, and everything else, it's easy to feel like you're constantly juggling a million things. If you're anything like me, making decisions can feel like navigating a maze blindfolded—stressful and totally exhausting. I used to struggle with decision-making big time. The simple act of choosing what to wear in the morning felt like a monumental task. It got to the point where I'd feel so paralyzed by indecision that I'd end up doing nothing at all.

What changed? I created and embraced a good routine. When you have a routine in place, all those little decisions suddenly become automatic, clearing mental space and removing unnecessary stress. Following a routine eliminates the guesswork from your day-to-day life. You know exactly what you need to do and when you need to do it, which means less time spent agonizing over choices and more time actually getting stuff done. It's like having a road map for your day—you know where you're going and how to get there—no GPS is required.

This chapter will explore the importance of a good routine, tips for setting one up, and what needs to be included. It will also discuss how mindful eating and good sleep can improve your stress levels. Finally, it will look at the importance of embracing journaling as part of your daily routine, so get ready to unlock the final puzzle piece for overcoming stress.

The Importance of Routine

Routines are more than just the mundane tasks you need to get done every single day. A good routine can make a huge difference in your life. Just look at the well-known, successful writer and producer Shonda Rhimes. She has admitted on various occasions that her strict morning routine is what allows her to be creative and productive. Chances are, if it weren't for her morning routine, we would not have had the joy of binging the hit television shows *Grey's Anatomy* and *Bridgerton* (Altrogge, 2022). While a routine helped Shonda achieve her goals, perhaps you should consider whether it can also be greatly beneficial to you.

Being spontaneous can feel exciting in certain areas of life, but if everything in your life depends on spontaneity, you'll feel uncertain and anxious. A routine provides stability, safety, and comfort, keeping you grounded and focused even when things feel busy and overwhelming. Routines also help you overcome barriers that might be preventing you from doing what needs to be done. Let's say you want to start your own business, but every day, you feel unmotivated to start. However, if it's scheduled into your routine to work on your business plan every day at 4 p.m., you are more likely to accomplish your goal.

A routine is also helpful because it encourages consistency and repetition, which means you'll get better at whatever it is you're working on. When you do something every day, you are sure to improve, which will boost your morale (Knights, 2024). Research has shown that when people have regular habits and processes in place, they spend less mental energy on the stuff they do every day.

This frees up space to be creative, think outside the box, and solve problems.

Routines are also good for your physical health, as they allow you to prioritize and make space in your day for the things that matter, such as healthy eating, exercise, and resting your mind. In other words, having a routine isn't just about making sure you don't forget to brush your teeth in the morning but about creating a framework that helps you manage stress and anxiety better. So, even though a routine might sound boring, it actually allows you more control and freedom to do the things you enjoy. Let's take a closer look at how to set up a routine that actually works.

Tips to Set Up a Routine

Creating a routine isn't always easy, especially if you want the routine to be realistic and have longevity. Many routines on the internet can be a little far-fetched or simply not realistic for your lifestyle. For a long time, I tried to embrace the routines of the people I saw online, but I soon realized it was impossible. Why? It's literally their job to live in those routines and post about them, whereas you and I might have slightly different priorities. To create a routine that actually works for you, let's take a look at a few tips and steps to make it happen:

Creating the Routine

1. First, start by mapping out what a typical week looks like for you. Grab a pen and paper and divide it into three columns: personal, work, and relationships. Under each heading, jot down everything you do in a typical week. Next, write down the things you'd like to do in a typical

week that might make your week more fulfilling and exciting.
2. Next, create a routine and plan your week by allocating specific days and time slots for everything you *need* to do that week. Next, add the things you would *like* to do in the time slots where you usually waste time or are stressed out. Remember to be flexible with your time slots, as you never know what might happen.
3. Finally, support your routine by making it a habit. As mentioned previously, if you would like to learn more about habits, I recommend reading *Atomic Habits* by James Clear. In the meantime, use the following tips to ensure your routine is sustainable and realistic.

Tips for a Morning Routine

A good morning routine can look different from person to person, but most routines include a few healthy building blocks. Here are five things every morning routine should include if you want to make your day a success (Altrogge, 2022):

- **Get up early:** This gives you more time in the morning to ease into the day, avoid rushing, and accomplish things that set you up for success.
- **Make your bed:** Starting your day with a small accomplishment can set a positive tone and instill a sense of order that carries over into other areas of your life.
- **Practice affirmations:** Affirmations are positive statements you repeat to yourself that can help boost confidence and focus on your goals. Saying them in the morning can prime your mind for a productive day. For example, "Today will be a good day."

- **Get moving:** Exercise, even a short burst in the morning, gets your blood flowing, wakes you up, and can improve your mood and energy levels throughout the day.
- **Take a shower:** A refreshing shower can help you feel more awake, energized, and ready to tackle the day. It can also be a time for self-care and a moment of mindfulness.

Tips for a Night Routine

Similarly to the morning routine, a few elements can elevate a good nighttime routine. Here are three things you should consider adding to your nighttime routine to unlock all of its benefits (Altrogge, 2022):

- **Reflect on the day:** Take some time to think about what happened during the day. This could involve journaling, meditating, or simply having a quiet conversation with yourself. Reflecting can help you process emotions, learn from experiences, and feel a sense of closure before bed.
- **Prepare for the morning:** Laying out clothes, packing your bag, or prepping breakfast the night before can save you precious time and mental energy in the often-rushed mornings. This allows you to start your day feeling calm and organized.
- **Clean up:** Tidying up your living space can reduce clutter and create a sense of calm before bed. You could put things away, do a light sweep of the kitchen, or simply make sure everything is in its designated spot.

Adding Mindful Eating to Your Routine

Stress can easily lead to overeating and emotional eating. When you are experiencing a lot of stress, your body is more likely to crave fatty, starchy, and sugary foods, which leads to unhealthy eating habits. Eating healthy isn't about starving yourself or trying to be a certain size; instead, it's about fueling your body appropriately for the task ahead. By having balanced eating as part of your routine, you are more likely to provide your body with the fuel it needs. But there's more to eating than just the actual food—it's also about how you eat. That's why you need to make mindful eating part of your routine.

One of the easiest ways to engage in mindful eating is to use the four S principles, as explained by Amit Sood (2013) in *The Mayo Clinic Guide to Stress-Free Living*:

- **Slow:** The first key point is to take your time and eat slowly. Remind yourself that there's no rush and the food won't run away from you.
- **Small:** Instead of shoving down large bites, be mindful about it and take small bites that you can really enjoy and taste.
- **Savor:** Enjoy the flavors and textures of your food, and savor the company of the people you're sharing your meal with.
- **Smart:** Make intelligent choices about what you eat. Opt for whole, unprocessed foods whenever possible or foods you know will satisfy your hunger.

There are also various other ways to add mindful eating to your routine, starting with eating on a regular schedule. When you skip mealtimes because you are stressed, you are more likely to binge on unhealthy snacks later in the day or to overeat during your next meal. By sticking to a schedule, you ensure that your hunger levels don't reach a point where you binge on anything you see. Eating regularly will also help you regulate your emotions, enabling you to deal with stress more effectively (Greenberg, 2016).

Another way to add mindful eating to your routine is by planning your meals. A lack of planning often leads to unhealthier options such as takeout. By planning ahead, you can ensure that you are eating balanced meals every day, and it will help you to avoid skipping meals when you're busy. It's important to be aware of the stressors that trigger you into a binge session since these triggers can prompt intense cravings and cause you to feel more stressed about the day.

Lastly, one of the best ways to ensure mindful eating is to limit your alcohol intake. Alcohol reduces your ability to make good decisions, which can lead to binge eating or opting for less healthy choices (Greenberg, 2016).

In other words, adding mindful eating to your routine is a great way to take care of your overall well-being and reduce subconscious stress.

Adding Proper Sleep Hygiene to Your Routine

Have you ever woken up after a night's sleep and felt even more tired than before? That might be due to poor sleep hygiene. However, poor sleep doesn't only mean a lack of sleep. You might spend a full eight hours in bed and still have poor sleep hygiene. Why? Because sleep is so much more than just the number of hours you spend in your bed. Poor sleep hygiene can heavily increase your stress levels, while proper sleep hygiene can effectively combat stress, helping you to wake up feeling relaxed and renewed. That's why it's crucial that you consider good sleep hygiene as part of your routine.

The first way you can ensure proper sleep hygiene is by assessing your sleeping hours. Studies have shown that adults need between six and nine hours of sleep a night, with females on the higher side of the scale and males on the lower side. Any less or more, and you risk serious health issues such as weakened immune systems and insomnia (Kripke et al., 2002). You can ensure good sleep hygiene by sticking to the same sleep and wake schedule. In other words, get up at the same time every day, even on weekends, and go to bed at the same time every night, even when you have work that needs to be done. By doing so, you program your brain and your body to automatically switch off at a certain time, allowing you to rest more effectively, as well as wake up more easily (Altrogge, 2022).

Temperature also plays a significant role in the quality of your sleep. Your body needs to cool down to fall asleep, which is why it's advised that you lower your thermostat before you get into bed. Studies have found that the ideal bedroom temperature is between 60-65 °F (Altrogge, 2022). You can also lower your temperature by sipping water before getting into bed and ensuring that you're not wearing clothes that might be too warm.

Blue light or a lack of complete darkness is another element that contributes to poor sleep hygiene. When you're in bed, it's tempting to grab your phone and scroll through Instagram or TikTok for a few minutes, but those few minutes of scrolling can negatively impact the quality of your sleep. When you spend too much time in your bed watching television or scrolling, your brain will begin to associate the bed with a time of being awake, making it harder to fall asleep.

If you find yourself in bed, unable to fall asleep for various reasons, try a progressive muscle relaxation technique, as discussed in chapter seven. This will allow your body and mind to relax, helping you to fall asleep and wake up feeling less anxious. By implementing all of these small techniques into your sleep routine, you are sure to feel less stressed and wake up feeling excited for the day ahead.

Adding Journaling to Your Routine

My husband used to be stressed constantly, and everything sent him into a tailspin—running late, waking up early, you name it. It got to the point where I knew something had to change. After much pleading, I convinced him to give journaling a go. I knew if I called it "journaling," he'd probably roll his eyes and give up before he even started. So, I changed my approach slightly. Before bed each night, I asked him to answer three questions:

- What were three positive things that happened today?
- What stressed you out?
- What could you have done to deal with those stressors?

At first, it was a bit of a struggle, but as he kept at it, he started noticing the change. Slowly but surely, he started to realize that many of his worries were way bigger in his head than they were in real life, and having those action plans written down gave him a road map for dealing with stress in the future. Within weeks, he struggled to find three things to mention that stressed him out because a lot of the weight was lifted off his shoulders. That is what journaling is all about and why it's an excellent addition to our daily routines.

Journaling isn't a one-size-fits-all, and there are many different approaches. The key is finding what works for you. Maybe you'll use a traditional pen-and-paper journal or an app on your phone. Regardless of the method, the benefits will remain the same. Speaking of which, let's discuss the benefits of journaling.

Firstly, journaling provides a safe space for you to express your emotions. It's like sharing your secrets with your best friend, knowing they will keep them safe. Journaling can provide the same relief, allowing you to express emotions without judgment. As seen in my husband's case, journaling is also a wonderful stress release.

Journaling is also a tool for problem-solving. By writing down your thoughts, you can see things from a different point of view. This will help you find a possible solution for the problem you're facing. That's why journaling is so powerful when it comes to mental health. It can help ease feelings of depression by interrupting those pesky negative thought patterns and giving you a new perspective on things. Journaling can also help boost your mood, set goals, and improve creativity. Here are a few tips and tricks to help you incorporate journaling into your routine:

- **Dedicate time and space:** Find a specific time in your day that works for you, whether it's early in the morning, during your lunch break, or at night. Once you find a time that works for you, stick to it and make it part of your schedule. You should also find a place that works for you. Make sure that you feel cozy and safe, and that you can journal without being interrupted.
- **Start small:** Don't start off with the expectation that you'll write pages and pages every single day. Begin small by asking yourself a few questions or simply writing down how you're feeling. Don't pressure yourself to fill a journal in a week (Wright, 2023).
- **Tell a friend:** Having someone to hold you accountable is a great way to ensure consistency. Tell a friend or a loved one that you trust about your journaling goals and give them permission to ask you whether you've journaled or not.
- **Forget about perfection:** Don't try to be perfect or create a beautiful journal. It can be messy and all over the place as long as it provides you with an outlet. Don't be hard on yourself, and don't worry about spelling. All you have to do is write what you feel.
- **Make it fun:** Make sure that journaling time is fun. Invest in a journal that you enjoy looking at and make use

of color if that's something you want. Don't see it as a chore; embrace the creative side of journaling and have fun with it (Wright, 2023).

With these tips, you'll be well on your way to incorporating journaling into your daily routine.

There you have it—the power of routine, nourishment, sleep, and journaling. By incorporating these habits into your daily life, you're not just checking off tasks—you're investing in your well-being. Raise a toast to the small changes that make a big difference, and commit to nurturing yourself—body, mind, and soul—one day at a time.

CONCLUSION

Can you believe you've reached the end of this book? It's been an honor to explore the potential of a stress-free world with you over the last 11 chapters. You dived into the depths of stress, explored its causes, and, most importantly, uncovered a treasure trove of strategies to combat it. To wrap up, I want to leave you with some final thoughts and encouragement to carry forward on your stress-busting adventure.

First and foremost, remember that you're not alone in this. Everyone experiences stress at some point in their lives, and it's completely normal to feel overwhelmed from time to time. Give yourself props for taking the initiative to tackle it head-on. You're already making strides just by being here and seeking ways to improve your well-being.

Throughout this book, I've emphasized the importance of self-awareness. Understanding what triggers your stress and how it manifests in your life is crucial to developing effective coping mechanisms. Take some time to reflect on your experiences, both past and present. What situations or circumstances tend to cause your stress levels to skyrocket? How do you typically respond when you're feeling overwhelmed? How would you like to manage your stress? By honing in on these insights, you'll be better equipped to respond proactively when stress rears its head.

One of the most valuable lessons you can learn is that you have more control over your thoughts and reactions than you often realize. Sure, life can throw you some curveballs, but it's how you choose to handle them that makes all the difference. So, when you find yourself in the midst of a stressful situation, try to take a step back and assess things from a broader perspective. Is this something that will matter a week from now? A month? A year? Chances are, many of the things you stress about daily are fleeting in the grand scheme of things. Focus your energy on what truly matters, and let go of the rest.

Of course, no discussion about combating stress would be complete without addressing the importance of self-care. Remember, you can't pour from an empty cup. Prioritize your physical and mental well-being by carving out time for activities that nourish your soul. Whether it's practicing mindfulness, engaging in creative outlets, or simply indulging in some much-needed rest and relaxation, make self-care a non-negotiable part of your routine.

Life is full of ups and downs, and learning to bounce back from adversity is a skill worth cultivating. Instead of viewing setbacks as insurmountable obstacles, see them as opportunities for learning and growth. Embrace the challenges that come your way with an attitude of curiosity and resilience. Remember, you've overcome every obstacle you've faced up until this point, and there's no reason to believe you won't continue to do so in the future.

Lastly, don't forget to lean on your support network. Whether it's family, friends, or a trusted mentor, having a strong support system can make all the difference when navigating life's challenges. Don't be afraid to reach out and ask for help when you need it. Vulnerability is not a sign of weakness but a testament to your strength and courage.

As you bid farewell to this book, I want to leave you with this reminder: You are capable, you are resilient, and you have everything you need within you to lead a happy, fulfilling life. Go forth with confidence, knowing you have the tools and the support to conquer whatever challenges come your way. Here's to a stress-free future filled with joy, peace, and endless possibilities!

NOTE FROM AUTHOR

Thank you for reading! I have thoroughly enjoyed writing this book, and truly hope you've enjoyed reading it, and found value in it. If you have, it would be greatly appreciated if you could head over to Amazon and leave a review. This really helps small publishers like myself be seen.

Simply scan this QR code with your phone, and you will be taken to the book's review page.

Alternatively, to leave a review:

- Head over to the book's page on Amazon or find it through your purchases.
- Scroll down towards the bottom of the page and click the button that says "Write a Customer Review".
- You can simply leave a star rating out of 5, or write a short review.

To get a free copy of the 30-day transformation journaling challenge workbook, visit https://subscribepage.io/transformation-journal or scan the QR code at the start of the book.

Thank you - your support is greatly appreciated!

REFERENCES

Ackerman, C. E. (2018, February 5). *21 emotion regulation worksheets & strategies.* PositivePsychology.com. https://positivepsychology.com/emotion-regulation-worksheets-strategies-dbt-skills/

Ada's Medical Knowledge Team. (2016). *Acute stress disorder.* Ada; Ada. https://ada.com/conditions/acute-stress-disorder/

Akimbekov, N. S., & Razzaque, M. S. (2021). Laughter therapy: A humor-induced hormonal intervention to reduce stress and anxiety. *Current Research in Physiology, 4*(4), 135–138. https://doi.org/10.1016/j.crphys.2021.04.002

Alternate nostril breathing: How & why to practice. (2022, September 7). Cleveland Clinic. https://health.clevelandclinic.org/alternate-nostril-breathing/

Altrogge, S. (2022, December 20). *12 morning and evening routines that will set up each day for success.* Zapier. https://zapier.com/blog/daily-routines/

Ansell, E. B., Rando, K., Tuit, K., Guarnaccia, J., & Sinha, R. (2012). Cumulative adversity and smaller gray matter volume in medial prefrontal, anterior cingulate, and insula regions. *Biological Psychiatry, 72*(1), 57–64. https://doi.org/10.1016/j.biopsych.2011.11.022

Arlinghaus, K. R., & Johnston, C. A. (2018). The importance of creating habits and routine. *American Journal of Lifestyle Medicine, 13*(2), 142–144. https://doi.org/10.1177/1559827618818044

Australian Psychological Society. (2022). *Stress.* Psychology.org.au. https://psychology.org.au/for-the-public/psychology-topics/stress

Azami, M., Shohani, M., Badfar, G., Nasirkandy, M., Kaikhavani, S., Rahmati, S., Modmeli, Y., & Soleymani, A. (2018). The effect of yoga on stress, anxiety, and depression in women. *International Journal of Preventive Medicine, 9*(1), 21. https://doi.org/10.4103/ijpvm.ijpvm_242_16

Berk, L. S., Tan, S. A., Fry, W. F., Napier, B. J., Lee, J. W., Hubbard, R. W., Lewis, J. E., & Eby, W. C. (1989). Neuroendocrine and stress hormone changes during mirthful laughter. *The American Journal of the Medical Sciences, 298*(6), 390–396. https://doi.org/10.1097/00000441-198912000-00006

Bhattacharya, S., Pandey, U. S., & Verma, N. S. (2002). Improvement in oxidative status with yogic breathing in young healthy males. *Indian Journal of Physiology and Pharmacology, 46*(3), 349–354. https://pubmed.ncbi.nlm.nih.gov/12613400/

Browne, S. J. (2021, May 14). *How the meditation technique, "wheel of awareness," can improve your well-being.* Forbes. https://www.forbes.com/sites/womensmedia/

2021/05/14/how-the-meditation-technique-wheel-of-awareness-can-improve-your-wellbeing/

Calma, D. (2022, November 21). *How to relieve stress with laughter: 6 expert-backed tips*. Well+Good. https://www.wellandgood.com/relieve-stress-with-laughter/

Charalambous, A., Giannakopoulou, M., Bozas, E., Marcou, Y., Kitsios, P., & Paikousis, L. (2016). Guided imagery and progressive muscle relaxation as a cluster of symptoms management intervention in patients receiving chemotherapy: A randomized control trial. *PLOS ONE, 11*(6), e0156911. https://doi.org/10.1371/journal.pone.0156911

Cherry, K. (2019). *5 surprising ways that stress affects your brain*. Verywell Mind. https://www.verywellmind.com/surprising-ways-that-stress-affects-your-brain-2795040

Cherry, K. (2022, September 2). *Benefits of mindfulness*. Verywell Mind. https://www.verywellmind.com/the-benefits-of-mindfulness-5205137

Chetty, S., Friedman, A. R., Taravosh-Lahn, K., Kirby, E. D., Mirescu, C., Guo, F., Krupik, D., Nicholas, A., Geraghty, A. C., Krishnamurthy, A., Tsai, M.-K. ., Covarrubias, D., Wong, A. T., Francis, D. D., Sapolsky, R. M., Palmer, T. D., Pleasure, D., & Kaufer, D. (2014). Stress and glucocorticoids promote oligodendrogenesis in the adult hippocampus. *Molecular Psychiatry, 19*(12), 1275–1283. https://doi.org/10.1038/mp.2013.190

Childs, E., & de Wit, H. (2014). Regular exercise is associated with emotional resilience to acute stress in healthy adults. *Frontiers in Physiology, 5*(161). https://doi.org/10.3389/fphys.2014.00161

Cleveland Clinic. (2017, March 1). *What happens when your immune system gets stressed out?* Cleveland Clinic. https://health.clevelandclinic.org/what-happens-when-your-immune-system-gets-stressed-out

Cleveland Clinic. (2022, September 6). *How to do the 4-7-8 breathing exercise*. Cleveland Clinic. https://health.clevelandclinic.org/4-7-8-breathing/

Cleveland Clinic. (2023a, January 6). *Pursed lip breathing: Technique, purpose & benefits*. Cleveland Clinic. https://my.clevelandclinic.org/health/treatments/9443-pursed-lip-breathing

Cleveland Clinic. (2023b, February 21). *Acute stress disorder*. Cleveland Clinic. https://my.clevelandclinic.org/health/diseases/24755-acute-stress-disorder

Cronkleton, E. (2021, May 4). *Yoga for stress: Breath, poses, and meditation to calm anxiety*. Healthline. https://www.healthline.com/health/fitness/yoga-for-stress

Davidson, B. (2018, April 30). *7 visualization techniques to calm your anxious mind*. NetCredit Blog. https://www.netcredit.com/blog/visualization-techniques-calm-anxious-mind/

Davis, M. T., Holmes, S. E., Pietrzak, R. H., & Esterlis, I. (2017). Neurobiology of chronic stress-related psychiatric disorders: Evidence from molecular imaging studies. *Chronic Stress, 1*. https://doi.org/10.1177/2470547017710916

Davis, T. (2023, November 20). *How visualization can benefit your well-being.* Www.psychologytoday.com. https://www.psychologytoday.com/us/blog/click-here-for-happiness/202308/how-visualization-can-benefit-your-well-being

Default Mode Network. (n.d.). Www.psychologytoday.com. https://www.psychologytoday.com/au/basics/default-mode-network

Dolbier, C. L., & Rush, T. E. (2012). Efficacy of abbreviated progressive muscle relaxation in a high-stress college sample. *International Journal of Stress Management, 19*(1), 48–68. https://doi.org/10.1037/a0027326

Dunbar, R. I. M., Baron, R., Frangou, A., Pearce, E., van Leeuwen, E. J. C., Stow, J., Partridge, G., MacDonald, I., Barra, V., & van Vugt, M. (2011). Social laughter is correlated with an elevated pain threshold. *Proceedings of the Royal Society B: Biological Sciences, 279*(1731), 1161–1167. https://doi.org/10.1098/rspb.2011.1373

Eda, N., Ito, H., & Akama, T. (2020). Beneficial effects of yoga stretching on salivary stress hormones and parasympathetic nerve activity. *Journal of Sports Science & Medicine, 19*(4), 695–702. https://www.ncbi.nlm.nih.gov/pmc/articles/PMC7675619/

Elmer, J. (2022, May 6). *Why are emotions so important?* Psych Central. https://psychcentral.com/lib/why-are-feelings-important#addressing-emotions

Ferguson, S. (2009, November 23). *STOP mindfulness: What is it?* Psych Central. https://psychcentral.com/health/4-quick-mindfulness-techniques#:~:text=The%20%E2%80%9CSTOP%E2%80%9D%20acronym%20stands%20for

Fleck, A. (2023, November 13). *Infographic: One in four young people in the world feels lonely.* Statista Daily Data. https://www.statista.com/chart/31243/respondents-who-feel-fairly-or-very-lonely/

Ford, B. Q., Lam, P., John, O. P., & Mauss, I. B. (2018). The psychological health benefits of accepting negative emotions and thoughts: Laboratory, diary, and longitudinal evidence. *Journal of Personality and Social Psychology, 115*(6), 1075–1092. https://doi.org/10.1037/pspp0000157

Fox, K. C. R., Nijeboer, S., Dixon, M. L., Floman, J. L., Ellamil, M., Rumak, S. P., Sedlmeier, P., & Christoff, K. (2014). Is meditation associated with altered brain structure? A systematic review and meta-analysis of morphometric neuroimaging in meditation practitioners. *Neuroscience & Biobehavioral Reviews, 43,* 48–73. https://doi.org/10.1016/j.neubiorev.2014.03.016

Garland, E. L., & Howard, M. O. (2018). Mindfulness-based treatment of addiction: current state of the field and envisioning the next wave of research. *Addiction Science & Clinical Practice, 13*(1). https://doi.org/10.1186/s13722-018-0115-3

Ginexi, E., Burke, E., & Shurtleff, D. (2022, June). *Meditation and mindfulness: What you need to know.* NCCIH. https://www.nccih.nih.gov/health/meditation-and-mindfulness-what-you-need-to-know

Goyal, M., Singh, S., Sibinga, E. M. S., Gould, N. F., Rowland-Seymour, A., Sharma, R., Berger, Z., Sleicher, D., Maron, D. D., Shihab, H. M., Ranasinghe, P. D., Linn, S., Saha, S., Bass, E. B., & Haythornthwaite, J. A. (2014). Meditation programs for psychological stress and well-being. *JAMA Internal Medicine*, *174*(3), 357. https://doi.org/10.1001/jamainternmed.2013.13018

Greenberg, M. (2017). *The Stress-Proof Brain*. New Harbinger Publications.

Grossman, P., Niemann, L., Schmidt, S., & Walach, H. (2004, July 1). *Mindfulness-based Stress Reduction and Health Benefits. A Meta-Analysis*. Journal of Psychosomatic Research. https://pubmed.ncbi.nlm.nih.gov/15256293/

Harvard Health Publishing. (2020, July 6). *Relaxation techniques: Breath control helps quell errant stress response - Harvard Health*. Harvard Health; Harvard Health. https://www.health.harvard.edu/mind-and-mood/relaxation-techniques-breath-control-helps-quell-errant-stress-response

Hopper, S. I., Murray, S. L., Ferrara, L. R., & Singleton, J. K. (2019). Effectiveness of diaphragmatic breathing for reducing physiological and psychological stress in adults. *JBI Database of Systematic Reviews and Implementation Reports*, *17*(9), 1855–1876. https://doi.org/10.11124/jbisrir-2017-003848

How five-finger breathing can bring on deep relaxation. (2023, January 27). Cleveland Clinic. https://health.clevelandclinic.org/five-finger-breathing/

How stress can rewire your brain. (2018, August 22). BrainFutures. https://www.brainfutures.org/blog/how-stress-can-rewire-your-brain/

Hsu, S. (2023, June 19). *The history of mindfulness: A comprehensive guide to cultivating inner calm and improving mental well-being*. Choosemuse.com. https://choosemuse.com/blogs/news/the-history-of-mindfulness-a-comprehensive-guide-to-cultivating-inner-calm-and-improving-mental-well-being

Hyer, M. M., Wegener, A. J., Targett, I., Dyer, S. K., & Neigh, G. N. (2023). Chronic stress beginning in adolescence decreases spatial memory following an acute inflammatory challenge in adulthood. *Behavioural Brain Research*, *442*, 114323. https://doi.org/10.1016/j.bbr.2023.114323

Inoue, K., Horwich, T., Bhatnagar, R., Bhatt, K., Goldwater, D., Seeman, T., & Watson, K. E. (2021). Urinary stress hormones, hypertension, and cardiovascular events: The multi-ethnic study of atherosclerosis. *Hypertension*, *78*(5). https://doi.org/10.1161/hypertensionaha.121.17618

Javed, D., & Mishra, S. (2022). Yoga practices in Social Anxiety Disorder (SAnD): A case report WSR to paruresis. *Journal of Ayurveda and Integrative Medicine*, *13*(3), 100622. https://doi.org/10.1016/j.jaim.2022.100622

Kasala, E. R., Bodduluru, L. N., Maneti, Y., & Thipparaboina, R. (2014). Effect of meditation on neurophysiological changes in stress mediated depression. *Complementary Therapies in Clinical Practice*, *20*(1), 74–80. https://doi.org/10.1016/j.ctcp.2013.10.001

Khalsa, D. S. (2015). Stress, meditation, and Alzheimer's disease prevention: Where the evidence stands. *Journal of Alzheimer's Disease, 48*(1), 1–12. https://doi.org/10.3233/jad-142766

Kiecolt-Glaser, J. K., Habash, D. L., Fagundes, C. P., Andridge, R., Peng, J., Malarkey, W. B., & Belury, M. A. (2015). Daily stressors, past depression, and metabolic responses to high-fat meals: A novel path to obesity. *Biological Psychiatry, 77*(7), 653–660. https://doi.org/10.1016/j.biopsych.2014.05.018

King of the jungle: How and why to practice lion's breath. (2023, April 19). Cleveland Clinic. https://health.clevelandclinic.org/lions-breath/

Knights, K. (2024). *The power of daily routines and how they help you stay happy and healthy.* Professional Academy. https://www.professionalacademy.com/blogs/the-power-of-daily-routines-and-how-they-help-you-stay-happy-and-healthy/#:~:text=Routines%20help%20to%20give%20you

Kripke, D. F., Garfinkel, L., Wingard, D. L., Klauber, M. R., & Marler, M. R. (2002). Mortality associated with sleep duration and insomnia. *Archives of General Psychiatry, 59*(2), 131. https://doi.org/10.1001/archpsyc.59.2.131

Kurth, F., Zsadanyi, S. E., & Luders, E. (2021). Reduced age-related gray matter loss in the subgenual cingulate cortex in long-term meditators. *Brain Imaging and Behavior.* https://doi.org/10.1007/s11682-021-00578-6

Lapierre, S., Baker, B., & Tanaka, H. (2019). Effects of mirthful laughter on pain tolerance: A randomized controlled investigation. *Journal of Bodywork and Movement Therapies, 23*(4). https://doi.org/10.1016/j.jbmt.2019.04.005

Lau, K. K. H., Randall, A. K., Duran, N. D., & Tao, C. (2019). Examining the effects of couples' real-time stress and coping processes on interaction quality: Language use as a mediator. *Frontiers in Psychology, 9.* https://doi.org/10.3389/fpsyg.2018.02598

Legg, T. J. (2020, May 28). *Visualization meditation: 5 exercises to try.* Healthline. https://www.healthline.com/health/visualization-meditation#color-breathing

León-Pérez, J. M., Cantero-Sánchez, F. J., Fernández-Canseco, Á., & León-Rubio, J. M. (2021). Effectiveness of a humor-based training for reducing employees' distress. *International Journal of Environmental Research and Public Health, 18*(21), 11177. https://doi.org/10.3390/ijerph182111177

Levine, G. N., Cohen, B. E., Commodore-Mensah, Y., Fleury, J., Huffman, J. C., Khalid, U., Labarthe, D. R., Lavretsky, H., Michos, E. D., Spatz, E. S., & Kubzansky, L. D. (2021). Psychological health, well-being, and the mind-heart-body connection: A scientific statement from the American heart association. *Circulation, 143*(10). https://doi.org/10.1161/cir.0000000000000947

Lewis, K. (2021, April 27). *Guided visualization: Dealing with stress.* National Institute of Mental Health (NIMH). https://www.nimh.nih.gov/news/media/2021/guided-visualization-dealing-with-stress

Lindberg, S. (2019, November 20). *Stress and weight gain: Understanding the connection.* Healthline; Healthline Media. https://www.healthline.com/health/stress/stress-and-weight-gain

Lindsay, E. K., Young, S., Brown, K. W., Smyth, J. M., & Creswell, J. D. (2019). Mindfulness training reduces loneliness and increases social contact in a randomized controlled trial. *Proceedings of the National Academy of Sciences, 116*(9), 3488–3493. https://doi.org/10.1073/pnas.1813588116

Lohr, J. (2015). Can visualizing your body doing something, such as moving your arm, help you complete the action? What part of the brain is involved? *Scientific American Mind, 26*(3), 72–72. https://doi.org/10.1038/scientificamerican mind0515-72a

Louie, D., Brook, K., & Frates, E. (2016). The Laughter Prescription. *American Journal of Lifestyle Medicine, 10*(4), 262–267. https://doi.org/10.1177/1559827614550279

Lutz, J., Herwig, U., Opialla, S., Hittmeyer, A., Jäncke, L., Rufer, M., Grosse Holtforth, M., & Brühl, A. B. (2013). Mindfulness and emotion regulation—an fMRI study. *Social Cognitive and Affective Neuroscience, 9*(6), 776–785. https://doi.org/10.1093/scan/nst043

Mackereth, P. A., & Tomlinson, L. (2010). Progressive muscle relaxation: a remarkable tool for therapists and patients. *Integrative Hypnotherapy*, 82–96. https://doi.org/10.1016/B978-0-7020-3082-6.00008-3

Marks, H. (2023, October 8). *Stress symptoms*. WebMD. https://www.webmd.com/balance/stress-management/stress-symptoms-effects_of-stress-on-the-body

Marshall, L. (2018, December 6). *Your brain on imagination: It's a lot like the real thing, study shows*. CU Boulder Today. https://www.colorado.edu/today/node/31511

Mayo Clinic Staff. (2022, August 3). *Exercise and stress: Get moving to manage stress*. Mayo Clinic. https://www.mayoclinic.org/healthy-lifestyle/stress-management/in-depth/exercise-and-stress/art-20044469

Mayo Clinic Staff. (2023, August 10). *Stress management*. Mayo Clinic. https://www.mayoclinic.org/healthy-lifestyle/stress-management/in-depth/stress-symptoms/art-20050987

McCloughan, L. J., Hanrahan, S. J., Anderson, R., & Halson, S. R. (2016). Psychological recovery: Progressive muscle relaxation (PMR), anxiety, and sleep in dancers. *Performance Enhancement & Health, 4*(1-2), 12–17. https://doi.org/10.1016/j.peh.2015.11.002

McKay, M., & West, A. (2016, November 8). *Teaching clients the art of emotion surfing through mindful acceptance*. New Harbinger Publications, Inc. https://www.newharbinger.com/blog/quick-tips-therapists/teaching-clients-the-art-of-emotion-surfing-through-mindful-acceptance/

Medina de Chazal, H., Del Buono, M. G., Keyser-Marcus, L., Ma, L., Moeller, F. G., Berrocal, D., & Abbate, A. (2018). Stress cardiomyopathy diagnosis and Treatment. *Journal of the American College of Cardiology, 72*(16), 1955–1971. https://doi.org/10.1016/j.jacc.2018.07.072

Meier, M., Wirz, L., Dickinson, P., & Pruessner, J. C. (2020). Laughter yoga reduces the cortisol response to acute stress in healthy individuals. *Stress*, *24*(1), 1–9. https://doi.org/10.1080/10253890.2020.1766018

Mindful. (2021, February 11). *Everyday mindfulness with Jon Kabat-Zinn*. Mindful. https://www.mindful.org/everyday-mindfulness-with-jon-kabat-zinn/

Moszeik, E. N., von Oertzen, T., & Renner, K.-H. (2020). Effectiveness of a short Yoga Nidra meditation on stress, sleep, and well-being in a large and diverse sample. *Current Psychology*, *41*. https://doi.org/10.1007/s12144-020-01042-2

Mullen, L. (n.d.). *Free your brain from stress*. Bella Online. https://www.bellaonline.com/articles/art305378.asp

Murphy, S. E., Clare O'Donoghue, M., Drazich, E. H. S., Blackwell, S. E., Christina Nobre, A., & Holmes, E. A. (2015). Imagining a brighter future: The effect of positive imagery training on mood, prospective mental imagery and emotional bias in older adults. *Psychiatry Research*, *230*(1), 36–43. https://doi.org/10.1016/j.psychres.2015.07.059

Naik, G. S., Gaur, G. S., & Pal, G. K. (2018). Effect of modified slow breathing exercise on perceived stress and basal cardiovascular parameters. *International Journal of Yoga*, *11*(1), 53–58. https://doi.org/10.4103/ijoy.IJOY_41_16

Neff, K. (2022, September 16). *A 15-minute practice to soften, soothe, and allow difficult emotions*. Mindful. https://www.mindful.org/a-15-minute-practice-to-soften-soothe-and-allow-difficult-emotions/

Orme-Johnson, D. W., & Barnes, V. A. (2014, May 1). *Effects of the transcendental meditation technique on trait anxiety: A meta-analysis of randomized controlled trials*. Journal of Alternative and Complementary Medicine (New York, N.Y.). https://pubmed.ncbi.nlm.nih.gov/24107199/

Pal, M. M. (2021). Glutamate: The master neurotransmitter and its implications in chronic stress and mood disorders. *Frontiers in Human Neuroscience*, *15*(15). https://doi.org/10.3389/fnhum.2021.722323

Pietrangelo, A. (2017, June 5). *The effects of stress on your body*. Healthline. https://www.healthline.com/health/stress/effects-on-body#Central-nervous-and-endocrine-systems

Puterman, E., Lin, J., Blackburn, E., O'Donovan, A., Adler, N., & Epel, E. (2010). The power of exercise: Buffering the effect of chronic stress on telomere length. *PLoS ONE*, *5*(5), e10837. https://doi.org/10.1371/journal.pone.0010837

Rees, B. L. (1995). Effect of relaxation with guided imagery on anxiety, depression, and self-esteem in primiparas. *Journal of Holistic Nursing*, *13*(3), 255–267. https://doi.org/10.1177/089801019501300307

Rindfleisch, J. A. (2014). *The healing benefits of humor and laughter*. Veterans Affairs. https://www.va.gov/WHOLEHEALTHLIBRARY/tools/healing-benefits-humor-laughter.asp#ref-13

Robbins, T. (2021, March 20). *Everything you must know about relationship stress*. Tonyrobbins.com. https://www.tonyrobbins.com/love-relationships/how-to-help-partner-in-times-of-stress/

Robinson, L., Smith, M., & Segal, J. (2018, December 28). *Laughter is the best medicine.* Help Guide. https://www.helpguide.org/articles/mental-health/laughter-is-the-best-medicine.htm

Rod, K. (2015). Observing the effects of mindfulness-based meditation on anxiety and depression in chronic pain patients. *Psychiatria Danubina, 27 Suppl 1,* S209-211. https://pubmed.ncbi.nlm.nih.gov/26417764/

Rubin, G. (2016, November 28). *The challenge of predicting what will make you happy in the future.* Www.linkedin.com. https://www.linkedin.com/pulse/challenge-predicting-what-make-you-happy-future-gretchen-rubin/

Saltsman, T. L., Seery, M. D., Ward, D. E., Radsvick, T. M., Panlilio, Z. A., Lamarche, V. M., & Kondrak, C. L. (2020). Facing the facets: No association between dispositional mindfulness facets and positive momentary stress responses during active stressors. *Personality and Social Psychology Bulletin, 47*(7), 014616722095689. https://doi.org/10.1177/0146167220956898

Santosa, A., Rosengren, A., Ramasundarahettige, C., Rangarajan, S., Chifamba, J., Lear, S. A., Poirier, P., Yeates, K. E., Yusuf, R., Orlandini, A., Weida, L., Sidong, L., Yibing, Z., Mohan, V., Kaur, M., Zatonska, K., Ismail, N., Lopez-Jaramillo, P., Iqbal, R., & Palileo-Villanueva, L. M. (2021). Psychosocial risk factors and cardiovascular disease and death in a population-based cohort from 21 low-, middle-, and high-income countries. *JAMA Network Open, 4*(12), e2138920. https://doi.org/10.1001/jamanetworkopen.2021.38920

Schenck, L. (2011, November 8). *8 basic characteristics of mindfulness.* Mindfulness Muse. https://www.mindfulnessmuse.com/mindfulness/8-basic-characteristics-of-mindfulness

Schneiderman, N., Ironson, G., & Siegel, S. D. (2005). Stress and health: Psychological, behavioral, and biological determinants. *Annual Review of Clinical Psychology, 1*(1), 607–628. https://doi.org/10.1146/annurev.clinpsy.1.102803.144141

Scott, E. (2020, March 27). *Is journaling an effective stress management tool?* Verywell Mind. https://www.verywellmind.com/the-benefits-of-journaling-for-stress-management-3144611

Shaw, A. J., & Lubetzky, A. V. (2021). A short bout of exercise with and without an immersive virtual reality game can reduce stress and anxiety in adolescents: A pilot randomized controlled trial. *Frontiers in Virtual Reality, 1.* https://doi.org/10.3389/frvir.2020.598506

Signs and symptoms of stress. (2022, March). Mind. https://www.mind.org.uk/information-support/types-of-mental-health-problems/stress/signs-and-symptoms-of-stress/

Sood, A. (2013). *The Mayo Clinic Guide to Stress-Free Living.* Hachette UK.

Sood, A., & Jones, D. T. (2013). On mind wandering, attention, brain networks, and meditation. *EXPLORE, 9*(3), 136–141. https://doi.org/10.1016/j.explore.2013.02.005

Star, K. (2022, March 10). *Visualization techniques can help manage your symptoms.*

Verywell Mind. https://www.verywellmind.com/visualization-for-relaxation-2584112

Sutton, J. (2018, January 26). *Progressive muscle relaxation (PMR): A positive psychology guide.* PositivePsychology.com. https://positivepsychology.com/progressive-muscle-relaxation-pmr/

Tawakol, A., Ishai, A., Takx, R. A., Figueroa, A. L., Ali, A., Kaiser, Y., Truong, Q. A., Solomon, C. J., Calcagno, C., Mani, V., Tang, C. Y., Mulder, W. J., Murrough, J. W., Hoffmann, U., Nahrendorf, M., Shin, L. M., Fayad, Z. A., & Pitman, R. K. (2017). Relation between resting amygdalar activity and cardiovascular events: a longitudinal and cohort study. *Lancet (London, England), 389*(10071), 834–845. https://doi.org/10.1016/S0140-6736(16)31714-7

Telles, S., Verma, S., Sharma, S. K., Gupta, R. K., & Balkrishna, A. (2017). Alternate-Nostril yoga breathing reduced blood pressure while increasing performance in a vigilance test. *Medical Science Monitor Basic Research, 23*, 392–398. https://doi.org/10.12659/msmbr.906502

Tusek, D., Church, J. M., & Fazio, V. W. (1997). Guided imagery as a coping strategy for perioperative patients. *AORN Journal, 66*(4), 644–649. https://doi.org/10.1016/s0001-2092(06)62917-7

Twain, M. (n.d.). *Mark Twain quotes.* Brainy Quote. https://www.brainyquote.com/quotes/mark_twain_100621

Velikova, S., & Nordtug, B. (2018). Self-guided positive imagery training: Effects beyond the emotions–a loreta study. *Frontiers in Human Neuroscience, 11.* https://doi.org/10.3389/fnhum.2017.00644

Walton, A. G. (2015, February 9). *7 ways meditation can actually change the brain.* Forbes. https://www.forbes.com/sites/alicegwalton/2015/02/09/7-ways-meditation-can-actually-change-the-brain/?sh=24a023571465

Webster, E. M. (2022). The impact of adverse childhood experiences on health and development in young children. *Global Pediatric Health, 9*(9). https://doi.org/10.1177/2333794x221078708

WomensMedia. (2021, May 14). *How the meditation technique, "wheel of awareness," can improve your well-being.* Forbes. https://www.forbes.com/sites/womensmedia/2021/05/14/how-the-meditation-technique-wheel-of-awareness-can-improve-your-wellbeing/?sh=3eb163533941

Woodyard, C. (2011). Exploring the therapeutic effects of yoga and its ability to increase quality of life. *International Journal of Yoga, 4*(2), 49–54. https://doi.org/10.4103/0973-6131.85485

Wright, K. W. (2023, August 17). *Journaling for beginners: How to get started in 10 steps.* Day One | Your Journal for Life. https://dayoneapp.com/blog/journaling/#h-the-benefits-of-keeping-a-journa

Yang, C.-C., Barrós-Loscertales, A., Li, M., Pinazo, D., Borchardt, V., Ávila, C., & Walter, M. (2019). Alterations in brain structure and amplitude of low-frequency after 8 weeks of mindfulness meditation training in meditation-naïve subjects. *Scientific Reports, 9*(1), 1–10. https://doi.org/10.1038/s41598-019-47470-4

Yaribeygi, H., Panahi, Y., Sahraei, H., Johnston, T. P., & Sahebkar, A. (2017). The impact of stress on body function: A review. *EXCLI Journal, 16*(1), 1057–1072. https://doi.org/10.17179/excli2017-480

Yim, J. (2016, July 1). *Therapeutic benefits of laughter in mental health: A theoretical review*. The Tohoku Journal of Experimental Medicine. https://pubmed.ncbi.nlm.nih.gov/27439375/

Printed in Great Britain
by Amazon